Live By Faith

Constantin Hateganu

WESTBOW
PRESS®
A DIVISION OF THOMAS NELSON
& ZONDERVAN

WestBow Press books may be ordered through booksellers or by contacting:

WestBow Press
A Division of Thomas Nelson & Zondervan
1663 Liberty Drive
Bloomington, IN 47403
www.westbowpress.com
1 (866) 928-1240

ISBN: 978-1-5127-1228-5 (sc)

Library of Congress Control Number: 2015914866

Print information available on the last page.

WestBow Press rev. date: 1/26/2016

Contents

Dedication

First I want to give all the glory to God, to my Lord Jesus Christ and to the Holy Spirit who inspire me and help me to write down on paper my testimony of faith.

To my wife Jenny who was on my side the right helper with encouragement in all my years of service.

To all my family and friends.

Foreword

From Genesis to Revelation we find God trying to bring his people in relationship with Him as was originally in the Garden of Eden. God is Holy and it was impossible for man to stand in the presence of God after he sinned. For this God reviled to Moses to build the tabernacle, the things in it, the ritual the sacrifices, and the way which the high priest need to come before the God to represents the people. Likewise, the temple was built in Jerusalem by King Solomon.

The tabernacle and temple were the type of church where God wanted to live. The court of the tabernacle represent the gathering unto the Lord. In the Holy place we have the table of the bread represents the body of Christ, the lampstand represents the work and the Holy Spirit and the altar represents the sacrifice of Christ and behind the second veil in the Holiest of All we have the ark of the covenant which represents the presence of the Lord and in the ark the testimony: the Aaron's rod which budded represents our death in Christ and resurrection with Him manna represents the grace of God without our efforts, the ten commandments represents our inability to meet the laws of God. When the Priest put blood on the mercy seat the sins of the priest and of the people were covered and God would see the blood and the priest would not die in the presence of God.

Through the grace of God the law which would have condemned us was covered by the blood of Jesus and now we have entrance into the Holiest of All, in presence of God.

People across the times looked to find methods to bring God in their midst and to live amongst them but were only left with rituals and tradition, and some are just fine with that, but God does not need experts in his work just wants us to follow His instructions every time we get close to Him. Jesus came to restore the relationship between Himself and man. Like in the days of old there was need for cleaning, in the same way we need cleaning to receive the power of the Holy Spirit. Only after our heart is purely clean we can become the temple of the Holy Spirit. The Holy Spirit is God, He helps us get in the presents of God and teaches us what God needs from us. It is sad that a lot of churches have remained only with the rituals, traditions and doings and do not look or care to find the presence of God which is the sweetest. This is why people have lost the willingness and drive of even going to church and do not have the power and the love of doing the will of God. The purpose of The Old Testament and New Testament from the time of Jesus Christ until our present church days, is to bring man into the presence of God.

Introduction

In this book I want so share some of my experiences which I had in my life through serving the Lord and parallel to this some teachings from the Word of God, which will help us better understand the testimony from each chapter in the book, in the light of God's Word.

Having a different life I say, with many experiences of repentance and seeing that when confessing to others, they were interested to know more. I had it upon my heart to write this book. For sure this book could have been written a long time ago, but every time I started to write I stopped for many reasons and the biggest reason being that I didn't want people to think that I'm writing it to promote myself in any way, never crossed my mind then or at the present time. In all things I want to bring Glory to God because He is the only One whom deserves it. Finally led by the Holy Spirit and my family, American and Romanian brothers in Christ which have heard some of the testimonies I have started again to write. The purpose of this book is first of all to give Praise to the Lord for all His doings and to show readers about God's grace and love and about the signs and wonders that follow God's children that live by faith. Encouraging all believers and mostly our youth and friends to experience a life by faith.

God was close to me from the time that I received Him as my personal savior. He healed me, gave me His Holy Spirit and is with me today. He kept His promise towards me, and I fight to remain close to Him till the end. May God put this same thought in you my dear reader to find the Lord and not a deceiving religion and when you find Him may you never let Him go. I promise you that He will give you first of all salvation and then peace and happiness will follow and all that you may need here on earth and in Eternity. Sometimes it is true that you have to pay a price, but do not turn back because I am telling you it is worth it. Every time you get closer to God, He will get closer to you and you will discover things and mysteries which you could not otherwise understand if had not passed through it.

Do not forget to find a church that believes in the New Testament baptism made in the name of the Father, Son, and the Holy Spirit, a church that experiences the baptism of the Holy Spirit and the gifts and the fruits of the Spirit. This will help you and your family to grow and to enjoy God's presence. If you do not have a Bible ask a believer from the church often times they have them to give away for friends or buy one and make time to read it daily. Do not be absent from the house of the Lord (church) this way you will know God more and He will bless you.

Chapter 1

The Most Wonderful Mother

> Then Pharaoh's daughter say to her, "Take this child
> away and nurse him for me, and I will give you your
> wages." So the woman took the child and nursed him."
>
> Exodus 2: 9

I was born in the peaceful village of Curpen, which lies within
the pulchritudinous country of Romania. More specifically in
Toplita, Hunedoara of Romania to be exact. Here is where my
wonderful parents Gheorghe and Ida lived with my family. They
were both modest people who lived as agriculturalists. Curpen
is a village situated on two very beautiful hills between the two
cities of Toplita and Hateg. The little country village had about
60 families. Many have questioned the difficult life style, "how
could people live there?" they would ask.

It appeared that these people had moved there because
they could work the land and were tree cutters other known as
foresters, and the area was covered by kilometers of forests all
around, so the people remained there to fulfill their life. The
wood they chopped was easy to push down the steep hills. Once
the wood reached the bottom of the hills the foresters would

transport the wood down the river. The village was so far from a main road and did not even have a road for cars. It would have been too expensive to build one, especially because there was no electricity. It was during this time that electricity was brought to many other villages surrounding areas except for Curpen.

Our village was a very complicated working environmental due to its steepness, and location between the hills. To assist with this complication almost every family had to own or borrow a donkey. They used this creature to support transporting heavy loads for things such as shopping to the nearest store which was up to ten kilometers or farther away. They even used the donkeys to take or bring things to and from the fields such as water from the rivers that flowed around the village. I remember from my childhood being amazed by the women caring water on their heads walking along side of the donkeys. Unfortunately the river from the village was not enough water for the need of villagers and their live stalk.

As far as the school was concerned the village had a school for elementary students...

Praise the Lord! I remember being in the class room with many of my peers. The room was well organized, the teachers sat us according to our grade: The first row was the first graders, the second row was the second graders, the third row was the third graders, and because our class went to the firth grade the fourth/fit rows were occupied by simply fourth graders. Medical assistance came once a year when they needed to vaccinate all the children in the village. Once I ran away from school because I was scared of getting shots, and to be certain that the medical assistance had left I hid till late at night in a wooden box.

As far as religion is concerned the people of the village were Orthodox. We had a church that was open once per month or less, depending on the priest's schedule. The village was only able to have service if the priest passed through, because he had several other churches to visit. On the contrary when the priest did come it was a big celebration. Everyone dressed in their best and gathered at the church. Although there was limited space inside, the people remained thankful because even if they didn't have a seat within the church they were still able to hear the sermon from outside.

At the hill skirts was the Cerna River, a river coming from the Poiana Ruscai mountains. Many times during the summer I would take off work and go to this river with the other children. In this river we would go fishing, and when I grew older we would catch fish by hand. Sometimes we could bring home kilograms of fish for the family to eat. Later the government decided to dig in the land to collect the water from Cerna River. They did this to provide more water for the company of Siderulgic Combinat of Hunedoara, and their surrounding population which had grown in size. Because of this several villages were moved from the valley of Cerna. This change became problematic on the people's way of living because we were now more isolated.

The work with the forest had ceased and slowly people were finding jobs elsewhere. Most of the men got jobs in the mines of Teliuc where my father was also employed. My father would not be able to do anything around the house because he would leave before dawn and return late at night. Just the women and children were left in the village to work the land. Slowly people began to move closer to their jobs as they could. Some moved toward the city of Hateg, others moved towards the city of Teliuc or Hunedoara.

With my father's hard work and dedication my father was able to save some money to buy a piece of land at Hateg. Together with my mother they laid a foundation were they began to build a home. My parents did not get to see their dreams come to a reality because my father became sick of silicosis a pulmonary lung disease. He received this lung disease from the dust of the mines. He suffered for several years and later died.

I remember that day being ten years old on a beautiful Easter Sunday. Spring was one of the most delightful seasons in our little country village. It was so pleasant to admire all the new forest leaves beginning to grow, and observe the lillies of the valley bloom. The village was full of apples, pears, prune, and weeping willow trees. The village was located in the middle of what looked like a horse shoe of hills and all the fragrances from the flowers of the trees remained there. In the Orthodox religion we believed that the Heavens were open at Easter and on that beautiful Easter Sunday my father went to Heaven.

My parent's believed in God, and always asked God's blessings at every meal when sitting down to eat. After my father became ill I would see him daily praying and reading the Bible and prayer books next to his bed. Before my father died he had a vision, he told my mother, "I see a beautiful sun and a beautiful flower garden" and he asked her if she sees it too, until his soul left his body. My mother was left a widow to take care of the house, and two children myself and my sister two years older than I. Many people told her to remarry to have help with the house work and as kids, I only remember because I was now a little older. My mother would tell them, "For sure I can find a man or a husband but I will never find a father for my children." even though she was young around thirty when my father died she never remarried. We saw her sacrifice her life for our home and our family, because of this we respected her all our lives.

When I graduated from the fourth grade in my hometown I was then sent to go with my sister to the fifth grade in the city of Toplita. It was about eight kilometers of walking, it was beautiful but very strenuous especially during the winter season. Sometimes when it snowed there was so much it covered the road making it more difficult to tell if you were still on the right track. And at night when walking from school I could hear wolves in the forest howling to the night. I would leave before daylight and return late night and often times the school principal would send us home early to make sure we could make it home ok.

Both of us myself and my sister Nuti, as I called her we would see our mother's hardship and we understood her struggles. My sister would help her cook and feed the animals. She would also take her food in the fields where she worked. While I would be taking the cows to pastures, gathering wood for the fire in the winter, while also cutting the grass to feed the animals. After finishing her housework my mother would then prepare for the market. She did this by making sour cream, cheese, fruit preserves, and not to forget she also took chickens, eggs and milk to the surrounding village markets. At these market's mine workers would come to purchase food for their families. With the money she earned she would buy other groceries that she needed. By doing this we were able to sustain ourselves. We remained one of the few families in the area and were able to build upon the foundation that my father had laid for our house.

I helped the professional homebuilders with our home from the beginning, because we did not have the money to pay others to help. Once the house was up we moved right in, even that we didn't have windows. I remember caring furniture on our backs for thirty kilometers from Curpen to Hateg. We took as much as each of us could carry as we walked those long kilometers. Half way toward our destination was a village called Silvas. There was a bus that came through the village although we could not afford to pay for the bus ticket nor would we be allowed to bring furniture on board. So we decided that we would walk the days and nights until we had completely moved into one of the rooms to live.

Once we finished moving in life was easier. I continued to attend school, for seventh and eighth grade in the city of Hateg. After finishing eight primary grades a lot of people advised me to go on to technician school and to get a career and to start working sooner. The high school I completed going to night school. I enrolled in the school of Uzina Victoria Calan where I did mechanical technician school for three years. This was one of the biggest factory in the area and had thousands of workers men and women from all the cities around. After I finished school I was able to get hired there and worked until I went in the army. With God's help we were able to finish the house were we could live like the rest of the people. I never regretted the hardship from my childhood that helped me later in life. My hardships have helped me be more mature in my way of thinking, and to have life experience to be able to teach others.

Looking back I am always reminded and I will never forget how my mother's sacrifices her life for our happiness.

A Faithful Mother

On the pages of the Holy Scriptures we find many wonderful mothers, and I would like to give one as an example, Jochebed the mother of Moses. She was from the people of Israel that have moved to Egypt from the land of Cannan because of

Amene, during the time of Joseph, whom became the economist of Pharaoh after he was sold by his brothers. After the death of Pharaoh, another Pharaoh took his throne, seeing that the Israelites were too many in number gave an order to the midwives to kill all male born babies through which Moses was destined to be killed also. God had another plan with this child and put upon the heart of his mother Jochebed whom loved her son, to make an Ark of bulrushes for him and place the baby in it and put on the Nile River.

She wanted to save his life. His sister was looking out for him from afar. The daughter of pharaoh finds the ark with the child in it, and although she knew the law that was given, God put compassion in her heart for this child and she took the child. Then the sister of Moses said to pharaoh's daughter should I go and call a nurse for you from the Hebrew women so she may nurse the child for you? Very interesting that she liked the child and did not put him to death and agrees to bring a nurse from the Hebrew women for him. Whom do you think this woman was? Jochebed the mother of the child.

Pharaoh's daughter said to her, "Take this child away and nurse him for me, and I will give you your wages". So the woman took the child and nursed him. (Exodus 2:9.)

There are many mothers today that have family or financial hardships, and they think maybe it's better for them to abort a child than to give birth and live a hard life. But is this the will of God? Jochebed with the hardship of the entire family and being slaves in Egypt and the law was given to have the babies killed, still believed in God and God saved him because he had a big plan with Moses. She did not know it at the time but found out later. She did not take care of the child for the pay of the princess, she cared for him because she had faith in the God that he will pay for all her work. Even though Moses grew and lived in the palace, he never forgot the work and teachings of his parents. He was used in a special way by God for the deliverance of the people of Israel from the slavery of the Egyptians. (Hebrews 11:23-29.) I believe that family was planned by God. (Genesis 1:28; 2:18-24.) When we have a good family we have a good church and a good nation. Here we have the balance. Today the family is hit from every direction like never before. This is some of them:

Divorce – fifty percent of marriages end up in divorce in U.S., and sixty percent in second marriages.

Abortions – over a million children are aborted per year in U.S., a child every 26 seconds, 137 children per hour, 3,300 children per day, 100,516 children per month, and 1,206,192 children per year.

Pornography – in the last several years the most harmful for the family and the church is pornography. This is the least talked about in public. And also sex before marriages and same-sex marriages.

Families Need Healing and Spiritual Awakening

The Apostle Paul tells the Ephesians and is telling us also: "Submitting to one another in the fear of God. Wives submit to your own husbands, as to the Lord. For the husband is the head of the wife, as also Christ is the head of the church, and he is the savior of the body. Therefore just as the church is subject to Chris, so let the wives be to their one husband in everything. Husbands love your wives, just as Christ also loved the church and gave Himself for he, that He might sanctify and cleanse her with the washing of water by the Word, that He might present her to Himself a glorious church, not having spot or wrinkle or any such thing, but that she should be holy and without blemish. So husbands ought to love their own wives as their own body; he who loves his wife loves himself."

Eph 5:21-28.

The Word of God teaches us, parents:

"Therefore hear, O Israel, and be careful to observe it, that it may be well with you, and that you may multiply greatly as the Lord God of your father has promised you – a land flowing with milk and honey. Hear, O Israel; The Lord our God the Lord is one! You shall love the Lord your God with all your heart, with all your soul, and with all your strength. And these words which I command you today shall be in your heart. You shall teach them diligently to your children, and shall talk of them when you sit in your house, when you walk by the way, when you lie down, and when you rise up. You shall bind them as a sign on your hand, and they shall be as frontlets between your eyes. You shall write them on the doorposts of your house and on your gates."

Deut 6:3-9.

The Word of God teaches children:

"Honor your father and your mother, that your days may be long upon the land which the Lord your God is giving you."

Exodus 20:12.

The Word of God say that divorce is not the will of God.

> "For this reason a man shall leave his father and mother and be joined to his wife, and the two shall became one flesh. So then, they are no longer two but one flesh. Therefore what God has joined together, let no man separate."
>
> Matt 19:5-6.

The Word of God teaches us about abortion:

> "You shall not murder."
>
> Deut 5:1.

> "But if any harm follows, then you shall give life for life."
>
> Exodus 21:23.

We need to pray to God to bring awakening to our families and our nation. We need to repent and ask God for forgiveness.

Amen!

> "For the mountains shall depart and the hills be removed, But My kindness shall not depart from you, Nor shall My covenant of peace be removed, Says the Lord, who has mercy on you."
>
> Isaiah 54:10.

Chapter 2

The Visions

"Now I saw a new heaven and a new Earth, for the
first heaven and the first Earth had passed away. Also
there was no more sea. Then I, John, saw the holy city,
New Jerusalem, coming down out of heaven from God,
prepared as a bride adorned for her husband. And I heard
a loud voice from heaven saying, "Behold, the tabernacle
of God is with men, and he will dwell with them, and
they shall be His people. God Himself will be with them
and be their God. And God will wipe away every tear
from their eyes; there shall be no more death, no sorrow,
nor crying. There shall be no more pain, for the former
things have passed away."

Revelation 21:1-4

A few years after I came home from the army, God allowed me
to go through a big trial in my life. During this trial I was very
desperate, to the point where life had no meaning to me and I
wanted to end my life. No matter how much people tried to calm
me down I still remained in desperation. Finally the moment
came where I was in my most desperate hours and God came

through to me and my prayers. He began working in my life through a co-worker and friend named Nelutu. Nelutu told me for the first time about God in detail.

He took me to a funeral in a village called Nalat, which was close to the city of Hateg, at which I lived. There I heard for the first time a sermon about the sacrifice of Jesus Christ. The pastor name was Dugulescu. He was a preacher who preached in Hateg and served in the church. Later in the years he served the church in the city of Timisoara, where God used him during the revolution of 1989 where he spoke to the people of Romania. The Lord blessed him through his sermons, and had everyone reciting The Lord's Prayer after him.

Once while accompanying Dugulescu on our journey home to Hateg he told me of the many miracles he had witnessed. He explained to me how he witnessed God work in his family and in his life. For example He testified about a time where he and his family were left without food. He immediately got down on his knees and prayed to God. Then the greatest thing had happened once he got off of his knees and stood, there was a knock at the door. When he opened the door a woman (his sister) walked in with a basket of groceries and told him that she felt led to bring these to the family. They rejoiced together and praised God because He had answered his prayers.

Similarity God had a plan for me. One day while I was working at the factory I had met a beautiful girl at the water well. I asked her to give me water and she was very happy to get water out and give me to drink. After that moment I realized that I had adored her. We became friends and after a few months got married and moved to the city of Deva where she lived with her parents. The thing that truly brought us together was that we both were moved by God's Word. We were soon looking to find a church where we could go to worship The Lord. We decided that every Sunday we would go to church to hear the Word of God. We decided to do this so that we may strengthen and straighten our lives after His will. We so much desired to see the miracles which He performed through his children.

The city of Deva used to be a closed city, because of this closure it was very difficult to get approval to live there. One could only get approval if you had found a job in the city's neighborhood. After a lot of searching we found a job at a concrete company. At this job we poured the concrete for foundations on residential buildings in the city. This job was a very strenuous, due to how many hours we were having to work. After a few months we prayed and took our identification paper to the official office and they gave us a visa to live in the city of Deva. They allowed us to live there without any questions, and they did not even looked at our visa. After that moment we saw the hand of God working in our lives and felt very blessed.

However the work was very laborious and after a short period of time I started to have pains in my back. Praise the Lord for hot showers! Every time I was in pain in my back from work I would return and allow the warm water to sooth my pain. One day when my pain had increased severely I had taken the bus to go home, however because it was so crowded it was very hard to even stand up. People noticed me in my pain, one person in particular had allowed me to lean against them. Once I arrived to my destination at the station I could barely make it home. Praise God that the station was not too far from home. As soon as I had arrived home I had told my wife that I wanted to take a hot shower because I was not filing well. She replied to me, "ok well I'm going to go get some groceries".

While I was taking my shower my pain had eased although when I got out immediately returned and grew in strength. I was able to make it into the bedroom to relax. After laying there on the bed I was unable to move my arms and legs. I remained palsied, with my entire body covered in heated shivers pain to the point where I had broken into a sweat. During this time I felt as if I was dying, I remembered praying and ask God to forgive me. I felt as if I was about to die and on my way to hell because I was not yet saved. It is true that I was going to church where I felt the presence of God. However we had never repented nor received a water baptism, the reason being because both my wife and I were pushing it off because we were young and thought that we had plenty of time to do that.

Now I was beginning to pray hard for God to forgive me. I had asked him, "If it be Your will Lord extend my life so that I could get water baptized and to be filled with the Holy Spirit". I assured him after I had become water baptized that he could do what he will with me, I just wanted to be saved. During this time as I was praying hard. My eyes were open and my soul was preparing for its rapture.

Then all of a sudden I saw a beautiful doubled door up in Heaven. On each side of the door it had two shiny gold hinges. Then all of a sudden the doors had opened and Jesus appeared in the doorway. I recognized Him immediately, His face was radiant with peace and joy. He was dressed in a special white robe reaching all the way to the floor. He motioned with both hands to go towards Him. How it happened I do not know but in a second I was with Jesus. Going through the passage of the doorway I could clearly see that there was a city. The City and all the things within it were full of life. It was so wonderful it seemed that all the things that were being said, were feeding me through peace and happiness. The walls were of crystal and you could see right through them. The city had some round posts which were all so alive in their colors. These colors from the posts ran from the bottom to the top and then again from the top to the bottom. Around the posts the colors would transform into a vapor or a smoke. The colors seemed like a rainbow surrounding all things in Heaven. In front I saw twenty-four thrones. These thrones were being reigned by someone and in the middle there was a taller throne. All of the thrones were surrounded by this rainbow that seemed to give off life to all of them and all things.

I could not see very well the faces of these people, it was as if they were covered by this vapor of smoke. Maybe it was not God's will for me to see their faces. Jesus took me to behind the thrones. When he walked I followed within his footsteps. I followed his every move, when He stood still so did I, it was like an impulse. It was interesting the next thing I remembered was whenever he had confronted a wall, a door would appeared that opened immediately without a door knob, or a handle. Jesus didn't even need to push it open, it simply opened by his presence. Once we entered through the door we came upon a beautiful garden. This garden was split into a division, one side there were fruit trees and on the other side was a flower garden. If you looked at the trees their flowers would change in color and in fragrance as well as their fruits. It was nothing that I had ever seen before, it was beyond miraculous. I saw here trees and flowers that I have not ever seen before and everything would be in a constant change and harmony that would give you a pleasant satisfaction. From behind the tall throne there was a beautiful valley continuing into a lush vegetation of beautiful grass. Something was telling me that there was a water spring.

Then Jesus told me that there is the spring of Life which will continue to flow to the Earth until His return.

Going forward I don't know how far I saw the nice hills against the horizon. Behind the hills was a bright light that was shining from a fire. The Lord then told me, "There is the lake of fire, where everybody who doesn't receive Jesus Christ on Earth nor repent for their sin, will be trow there". After we went around in the city I was thinking in my mind I have the feeling that I want to live there forever, I don't want to come back on Earth because was very beautiful in the Lord presence. But Jesus told me that, "You need to return to Earth, you need to tell to many nation what you hear and what you see here, and with you I have a missions on Earth and many will turn with their heart to me and repent, and you will come back here in your time on the place I prepaid for you and for all which they do my will on Earth." After He told me these words instantly I came back to my body and I start to feel the pain run through my entire body once again.

In few hours my wife came back home, once she entered into our bedroom she bowed on her knees and started to pray for me. When she was praying God used my mouth and speak she heard the words "You are healed" come from my mouth, my wife stop praying and looked on me with wonder. Her eyes gazed at mine wondering what might have happened. I too wondered what had just happened after God use my mouth and speak. After The Lord used my mouth to say, "you are healed" the pain was gone. I then tried to move my hand, my feet, my head, and I move them with no more pain. Glory be to God! I was healed. I thrower the blanket on the side and everything on the bed was filled with water from my sweat and tears. We stayed up all night testifying to one another on what God did for me. I told my wife what He showed me, about eternal life and my purpose here on Earth. If before I was crying for forgiveness, now I was crying of happiness because God had mercy on me. He healed me and gave me the possibility to get what I ask for to get baptized and get the Holy Ghost and serve the Lord for the rest of my life through His time and plan.

God's Plan Through Faith

In the beginning God planted a garden in Eden, and from the ground the Lord God made tree grow that is pleasant to the sight and good for food. The tree of life was also in the midst of the garden, and the tree of knowledge of good and evil. God put Adam and Eve after He created on the garden to tent and keep it. And the Lord God commanded the man, saying, "Of every tree of the garden you may freely eat, but of the tree of the knowledge of good and evil you shall not eat, for in that day that you eat of it you shall surely die."

Gen 2:15-17.

The Lord God walking in the garden in the cool of the day to have a fellowship with the man He created. The serpent was more cunning than any beast of the field which the Lord had made and he come to the woman and make her eat from forbidden fruit and she gave it to her husband and he ate it too. The eyes of them were open and they knew that they were naked. Disobedience to the commandment of the Lord by the sin committed has brought physical death of the body and spiritual death separation from God so death passed open all man as the psalmist says" Behold, I was shape in iniquity, and in sin my mother conceived me."

Ps 51:5.

From Genesis to Revelation we find God trying to bring back the man in the fellowship with Him as was in the Garden of Eden. Because the man is sinful and God is holy now was impossible for man to enter in the presence of God for the sin made separation between God and man. For this the sin need to be remove. And God in His love has uncovered a plan to Moses to build a tabernacle, the priesthood and the sacrifice to cover the sin. All of this thinks were a shadow of the think's to come which had its fulfillment in church age in the Lord Jesus.

The tabernacle represent the church where God wants to live, the bread table represent the Lord's body the candlestick represent the Word of God and the Holy Spirit, the altar represent the Lord sacrifice, the yard represent God assembly, the ark of the covenant represent the presence of God, and the thinks from the ark: Aron rod that budded represent our death with Christ and our resurrection with Him our born again, manna represent the grace of God without our work, the ten commandments talk about our inability to keep the law of God. When the priest sprinkled blood on the mercy seat of the Ark of the Covenant the sins were covered with the blood and the Lord see the blood and the priest don't die in the Lord presence. The law which condemns us was covered with the blood of the Lord and now we have free entry in the presence of the Lord in the Most Holy place.

People across the ages and looked to find ways to bring God into their midst to live with them but they remained only with rituals and customs and they remain empty. Many are happy with it because they don't know another way, and others are still looking. The Lord Jesus will come again to restore the relationship between man and God through His sacrifice. He brings the good news of preaching the Gospel after which the people have the opportunity through faith and repentance to receive forgiveness of sins come close to God through water baptism and Holy Spirit baptism. The Holy Spirit teach us how to please God and help us to enter in the presence of God. Our beloved Heaven and treacherous Hell are a true reality, we have evidence on the pages of the Scripture and of thousands of people who had revelations about it like me.

Heaven: (Paradise):

> And Jesus say to him: "Assuredly, I say to you, today you will be with Me in Paradise."
>
> Luke 23:43.

> "To him who overcomes I will give to eat from the tree of life, which is in the midst of the Paradise of God."
>
> Rev 2:7.

Hell:

> "These two were cast alive into the lake of fire burning with brimstone."
>
> Rev 19:20.

> "Then the Death and the Hades were cast in to the lake of fire. This is the second death."
>
> Rev 20:14.

The Lord Jesus tells us a parable in the Bok of Luke 15 :

"A certain man had two sons. And the younger of them said to his father, give me the portion of goods that fails to me. So he divided to them his livelihood. And not many days after the younger son gathered all together journeyed to a far country and there wasted his possessions with prodigal living. But after he spend all, there arose a severe fAmene in the land and he began to be in want. Then he went and join himself to a citizen of that country and he send him to the field and feed the pigs. He gladly want to fill the stomach with the pods that pigs eat but they don't give him anything. But he come to himself, he said, how many of my father's hired servants have bread enough and to spare and I perish with hunger. I will arise and go to my father, and will say to him, Father I have sinned against heaven and before you, and I am no longer worthy to be called your son. Make me like one of yours hired servants. And he arose and come to his father. But when he was still a great way off, his father saw him and had compassion and ran and fell on his neck and kissed him. And the son said to him, father I have sinned against heaven and against your sight, and am no longer worthy to be called your son. But the father said to his servants, Bring out the best robe and put on him and put a ring on his hand and sandals on his feet. And bring the fatted calf here and kill it, and let us eat and be merry for this my son was dead and is alive again, he was lost and is found. And began to be merry."

Luke 15:11-24.

This parable had many interpretation. If we look close to this younger son we see three things that led him to fall: The first things he never had the patience to sick family life and wanted to live his life as he like. The second he lived a prodigal life without parental control. The third and final interpretation was that all his possessions and began to starve. How long did he have his money and his friends when he spent everything left him, and he woke up only when he was feeding the swine and he was torment with hunger. This is the work of the sin first is seems sweet but after you do it for so long you became enslaved to it. The good news is, you can return to your father any time the sooner is better. If you are away from God, and you live in sin, the sin control your life maybe not like this prodigal son, but even the smallest of sins leads one to their death.

We note three things to return of this son: First he come to himself verse 17. This was his turning point, and before you come to God you need to come to yourself to see your situation, where the sin bring you. The second was his repentance he was sorry for himself, for what he did, verse 18 - I will arise and go to my father and I will say to him: Father I have sinned against heaven and against you and I am no longer worthy to be called your son. The third was his return. After he come to himself, after he repented in his heart he don't send the news, he don't send the letter to his father to forgive him but he himself rise up and go home. When the father saw him he run before him and kiss him. The father said to his servants, bring forth the best robe and put on him, put a ring on his finger and sandals on his feet's, and bring the fatted calf, kill it and let us eat and be merry my son was dead and is alive again, he was lost and he is found. And they began to be merry.

The same our Father in heaven enjoy when the prodigal son like us return home, and He receive us with the open arms. He will cover us with the robe of righteousness, and He put the engagement ring in our finger, and give us the sandal the zeal of the Gospel, and He is ready to cut the fatted calf for His son wedding. Are you ready, you come to yourself, you repent, you return home yet if not, don't stay to long God love you He did everything for you and is waiting with the arm open.

Amen!

"Behold, I stand at the door and knock. If anyone hears my voice and opens the door I will come in to him and dine with him and he with me."

Rev 3: 20

Chapter 3

Baptism with the Holy Spirit

"When the Day of Pentecost has fully come, they were all with one accord in one place. And suddenly there came a sound from heaven, as of a rushing mighty wind, and it filled the whole house where they were siting. Then there appeared to them divided tongues, as of fire, and one sat upon each of them. And they were all filled with the Holy Spirit and began to speak with other tongues, as the Spirit gave them utterance."

Acts 2:1-4

After the vision, the news go fast to the city and brothers came with cassette player to record my testimony and to carry the message further. We were glad and gave glory to God every time. My wish was to be baptized as soon as possible. So I went to talk to the church ministry leaders and asked them to give me a water baptism. They were very happy to hear my wishes and they quickly wrote our names down on their list and promised my wife and I that they will be baptized on the first baptism to be held in the church. We regularly attended church, and we went to the prayer meetings in the evenings that were held by families during week. We also saw how God worked through the Holy Spirit. Many times when we would have a prayer meeting I would ask God to baptize me with the Holy Spirit. I asked him to do this that way no one else would know, and I would immediately receive a special feeling.

One Sunday morning when my wife and I were dressing for church my wife had hear a message from the Lord warning her that she would be feeling warm to have on the prayer meeting and that is exactly what happened. Most of the time we go home after church but this Sunday when we left the church with some brothers of Christ. They had invited us to have prayer in their house because some other brotherly friends from another town where coming to also visit them who were God vessels. Because we didn't have too much time to go back and forth from home back to church, we had decided to go straight to the prayer meeting.

In the beginning of the first prayer one brother who was a prophet had a revelation for us. He did not know us, in fact we met him for the first time at the prayer meeting. The prophet had said that the Lord had plans to baptize us with the Holy Spirit even in that day, and the prophet asked us if we believed enough to pray together for it. We responded in agreement, and we were beyond glad to ask God for this gift. We made a prayer which lasted about three hours in which I was baptized with the Holy Spirit with speaking in tongues me and my wife. I do not know how much time our brother stayed in prayer with us, or what they did, if they sat on his knees three hours or stood up and sang, but we were in the presence of the Lord. Praise Him in his glorious name!

We went straight to the church service in the afternoon after our prayer meeting. My wife and I were both very happy that the Lord had baptized us with the Holy Spirit. We loved to pray and we prayed everywhere to feel the presence of the Lord. We would also pray through the Holy Spirit. Not after many days I learned that in a village of Vetel near Deva were believers and an old brother is a vessel of the Lord which makes the baptisms in Mures River.

I talked to our brothers and I decided to go to Vetel to make contact with this brother to give us the baptism in the Mures River, we wanted to make sure it is as Scripture say in the river. The church then told us that they were not ready to do it unto they get more people. We want to be ready to go to heaven when the Lord came for His church. So together we went to the bus station out right in front of us, we made a signal with our hands to stop a car, but no body stopped. Finally later a small car stop next to us and they take us. In a car I saw two young people in love which were very busy with one another and didn't give us to much attention.

When we reached our destination where we wanted to go to Vetel, the driver asks her young friend, "Where we are going?" We suppose we will be going to Sibiu and not to Arad where actually going, they ask us where we want to go and I tell them we are right there, they live down, and turn the car back to Sibiu where actually wanted to go and we saw how God take care of us and praising Him.

Brothers was waiting for us and together we went to the river Mures, where with the help of God and His servant we was baptized. There on roads and mud we put on our knees down and thanked God which helped us to make the holy covenant and said, Lord now you can take us home. After he prayed for us and had a word from the Lord for us. He gave several instructions then he lifted us in the arm of the Lord and left, and we return home full with holy joy.

We are filled with love for the Lord, and we confess His word everywhere. We confess the way of his salvation, and everything what He did for me. One evening a Brother named Mitru. Mitru was our brotherly neighbor who we would often pray together with. He comes to us and tells me that the Lord reveled something to him. He has given me the gift of healing. He tells me The Lord sends him to me and ask me to pray for my wife who is sick with cancer. She lies in bed for longest amounts of time. Then filled with holy fear I take my wife and I went to the Brother Mitru's apartment and find his wife lying in bed with lots of pain but she was very happy to see us. She did not know anything about our conversation and I told her that we have come to pray to God. We told her that He can heal her and reassured her that, at the same time that I talk, God will fill me with a greater faith. Then I fill the presence of the room with the Holy Spirit. I told her that I know she will be healed.

I was not too familiar with the word and I didn't known from where to read from, but I ask the Holy Spirit to guide me. Most of the time I open the Bible through faith to read, thinking God knows better than I what is needed for me to read. I then asked everybody to stand up to read the Word of God. We then stood for the reading the word, but only our sister was sick in bed.

I opened the Bible and the Bible opened to the woman with the spirit of divination of Acts16: 16.which cried after Paul and I instinctively closed the Bible, I tried to open it again and open in the same place, I closed it again now the third time trembling opened it, and opened in the same place, then I realized that God actually wanted me to read the text that to release the healing. Trembling and fearful I read the text and we all put our knees down and pray for this sister healing, and during prayer she was cured jumped out of bed and started crying. We all together began to glorify God. We all began to speak in tongues and to prophesy. It was a special presence of the Holy Spirit and filled all of us, and with joy we gave glory to the Lord for His love and His mercy.

Even if I moved to city of Deva, when I have opportunity I went to Hateg with joy to see my mother, my sister, her family, and to visit my wife brothers which live in Hateg to, and every time we visit our breather in Christ and the Pentecostal Church. One time when I visited the church they invite me to seat in the first bench out of respect of their personal guest. And when the pastor was preaching the Word of God I heard a voice of a man behind me shouting Halleluiah or Hosanna that moved me very much. I thought when the service is over I will go quickly to the exit door to find this man and talk to him.

So I did exactly this, when the service was over I looked over the people and saw this special man outside of the church. I was running out to make sure I didn't lose him, and when I meet him I was filled with a sense of respect for him. I shook hands with him and I asked him many questions. I asked his name, where he coming from, where he is going... and to all my questions he gave me biblical answers that pierced my heart. I asked him if we can walk together thinking, for sure he is not local and is going to the bus station, looking to know him more on the way. He agreed to let me walk by his side to get to know him a little better. The man was dressed up modestly in a blue working suit freshly washed. When the first time I saw him I wanted to give him some money in the name of Jesus, I put my hand in my pocket and took some money thinking when I tell him goodbye and shake his hand and give him peace I will give him the money in his hand and go. And really when we split up and shook his hand trying to give him the money he refused. I was surprised that this brother gave me back the money saying, that his father is rich, he has everything it needs and to keep the money for somebody who is in more need.

His behavior, his wisdom, his humility, his knowledge of the Word of God, and his responses gave me the feeling that I was talking with an angel sent by God to lead me. We stopped by my mother's house for nearly an hour until we needed to head toward the bus station. Once we arrived at the station we prepared to take the bus to our city Deva. When we reached the bus station there he was confessing the Word of the Lord without fear that may be detained and spoke about the love of God and many people were around him to hear. All of those things strengthened me. Everywhere I went I confessed the Word of God. No matter where I was, even on site where I was working, on break time, I would bring the people together. I would Bring the teams from plumbing, and the teams from construction. The reason I was able to bring everyone together was because I was a friend with their boss who was one of the leaders of the communist party on the company. One time I took him to church and together we preached the Word of God, praying and singing.

However not everyone enjoyed what we were doing, after some time had passed with our praise reaching the heavens someone had complained to the police. They called us to the police station the in the city of Deva one Sunday morning at 9 am. This was the time where we were supposed to be praising in church. I went to the station with my wife and my daughter. The police called us in one by one. They showed us some stairs that went down, they say there is a temporary jail where they throw all the people who break the law there. The police had then warned us to stop preaching on the job and if we continue to do so, they will put us in jail, and nobody can take us out from there not even God.

They warned us one more time saying you have a church where you can go to pray and sing. So we left the station with our warning, and continues on our day. Apparently they had connection to the site where we work and to punish us they began to send us to work from one city to another. The funny thing about this punishment was that, it was a blessing because we make fiends everywhere and we work hard to finish our job and look for brothers and sisters in Christ who want to pray and study the Word of God. If we don't find brothers in the area we walk on hills and valleys to find people at work. If we find the hungry souls, hungry to hear the Word of God we agree to assist them with their job.

While we help them complete their tasks at work we begin to share the love of God. As we continue to share we begin to praise, pray, and sing to the glory to the most High. At the end of the evening we bestow upon them a gift. The gift is a Bible so that the Word of the Lord can over flow within our new friends lives. Our new friends thank us with joy and happiness as they begin to kiss the Bible, they explain that they have never had not read the Bible. They claim that only the priest have such things.

I heard my mom was sick with a kidney stone, and she was in the hospital. I took my wife and I went to see her at the hospital. I decided I was going to testify the Word of God to her. The doctor said that she had a stone în both kidneys. The doctor mentioned that one Kidney is already locked and not working, and they need to put her on strong medicine because if the second kidney locks then they need to put her for surgery if not she will die.

I tell my mother, everything happens for a reason, even this sickness.

I remind her may it be for the glory God if we believe in Jesus then we must repent our sins to him. He is ready to heal us and you mother. So we all gather together and we pray for her healing. After our prayers we left to go home. The next day when I called my sister from Hateg to ask about my mother she told me in that morning my mother's kidney stone was no more. My sister told me that the doctor will let her come home. Then I thanked God for his love. Mother didn't get baptized right away, she decided that she wanted to keep her faith in her heart. The reason being because she don't want to give more problem to my sister and brother-in-law who work for telecommunications. After a few years she managed to take the baptism and the Lord gave her the gift of prophecy praise Him.

There was a time when we worked at a construction company local in our town to build four floored apartments. When I was working there I was a manager for plumbing. I also had a team that worked for me. Every day I was confessing the Word of God to fellow team members especially when we were on break. One night a coworker had a dream about God's judgment. She had decided to share it with as many people as possible. She said in the dream everyone gathered in a very large stadium. In the middle of the stadium was something like a big elevator. She said that when the Lorde called everyone by name that he would read their sentence.

Depending on each name that was sentenced the elevator took either went up to heaven or down to hell. What determined the direction up to heaven or down to hell was depending on who they served the Lord or Satan. When my coworker heard her name she said that in her dream that she began to cry and beg for forgiveness to the Lord. She said to herself I don't have time to repent I just heard the Word of God! She claimed that in her dream After the Lord spoke her name she began pointing to those who had testified to her, "pleading for more time to become a true believer she just kept pointing, saying, ive only recently heard about the word". In those emotions she said that she woke up crying and to find out, it was only a dream. That moment she gave glory to Lord because it was only a dream, and not reality.

My coworker then knew she had plenty of time to repent all of her sins. As she shared her dream with other coworkers their hearts where all touched one by one as they came to church with me. They were amazed by the things they had seen, considering they only heard negativity about the church.

During one of my journeys, I had went to a valley near Onesti. In fact my father had come to live here with this parents. The reason we set on a journey to this location was because a man who we knew lived here was living a very sinful life. You see the man was an alcoholic who kept and consumed too much wine. The man was also a heavy smoker who refused to give up and also refused to repent. So I went there with my wife to visit him, and every day I would teach him and tell him about God's love. I would tell him about and Jesus who was sacrificed his own life on the cross of Calvary for all of our sins. Although the man had a good friend who had seen him more often. The two of them would tell each other stories from their life, they would drink, they would smoke and they'd have fun. The reason why my father-in-law's drinking seemed everlasting was because he had his own winery where he would make his own wine. That why it was so easy for him to go more toward the wrong direction.

When we had gone to visit my father-in-law, his friend had also come to see him. My father-in law then had decided to start a fire inside to warm us up from the cold, when he had stepped out of the room, he had returned with a bottle of wine made from his vineyard. As the two of them were both drinking I confessed to them the Word of God. I told them about God's love as he gave his only begotten son Jesus to come and die for our sins. I told them we now have to repent to accept Him in our hearts to escape the judgment of God. After we had repented all of our sins to the Lord we decided to praise the Lord with a song. Once we were through singing our songs we prayed for them and left.

A few days later my father-in-law had promised us that he will come home after he finished some business. However I didn't believe him because time after time he had made promises to us but he never returned nor showed up. It was very hard for him to leave his friends. Once the Christmas season came we were all very surprised to see that he had actually come home like he promised. We were all so over joyed and happy that he finally kept his word and came home. After we exchanged some words he started to tell us what changed his heart to make the decision to come home.

He said, soon after we left those few nights ago his best friend had had a dream. In the dream the angel of death had dressed in black with his head covering his head, all of a sudden the angel of death and started to come closer to him in a very scary manner. The closer the angel came the more clearly his friend noticed that the angel had something in his hand. Then my father-in-law's best friend, said that he saw the Angel of death holding a giant book in his hand. The angel had a very strong and loud voice telling him to sign in the book, because it was his time to go. All of a sudden the angel hit his hand with a pen and repeated his request saying to sign. But the man refused once.

The death angel hit and yelled at the man a second time, third time, on the fourth time of being told to sign the book, he remember that there are more older people in the valley including his mother. He then told the Angel " I'm not the oldest one, go to them first". The man named three of them including his mother. He then requested the Angel to get them all first and after that then the angel of death could return to take him. Then all of a sudden the man awoke from his sleep, and ran to tell my father-in-law. After he told my father-in-law they decided to drink and talk about the dream to one another. But the next day after my father-in-law said that heard the church bells ringing. My father-in-law almost forget about his friend's dream, but when he asked some neighbors who had died, when they had mentioned that the mother of my friend die my father-in-law began to feel very weak. After few days the others two people named by my friend had also died, however when my father-in-law's friend died too, he said that he then became very scared because everything was happening exactly how his friend's dream had been described.

My father-in-law said that he now understands that this was not only a dream, but it was a reality. More specifically this reality is a sign from God for him to repent. My father-in-law then said that he took an axe and cut all of his wine containers, and let the wine spill to the ground so nobody can drink it. He then said goodbye to his neighbor, his friends, and packed his things and returned home with our family. Yes he left behind all the wine and cigarettes, and he decided to come to church to get baptized.

The Lord later made him a wonderful servant. He has come to us plenty of times saying that he had wished he had come sooner to Christ. He wishes that he would have come to meet Christ earlier because he spends so much of his days studying and analyzing the word. When some brothers come for me to go on some missions he was all ready by the door with his shoes. He was for me not only a father-in-law but was like a brother, and a good friend. I left him In Romania when I came over the border. The last years of his life he spent doing good things. He assisted many poor families who were less fortunate than himself, especially those with lots of children. He would always be giving everything he had because he knew he had given himself to the Lord. He had always set such a good example, and will had been a blessing to all that knew him. The Lord changed his life, he was born again, and if God changed him He can change you too.

The Holy Spirit

I believe in a Trinity of God; Father, Son and the Holy Spirit. The Holy Spirit is the power of God. He was on the beginning with God we find Him in Genesis 1:2. The earth was without form, and void; and darkness was on the face on the deep. And the Spirit of God was hovering over the face of the waters. He was the one He guided the prophets of the Old and New Testament and the last book of the Bible.

"And the spirit and the bride say, Come! And let him who hears say, Come! And let him who thirsts come. Whoever desires, let him take the water of life freely."

Rev 22:17.

"When our Lord was baptized by John in Jordan river the trinity was present: When He was baptized, Jesus come up immediately from the water; and behold, the heavens were opened to Him, and He saw the Spirit of God descending like a dove and alighting upon Him, and suddenly a voice came from heaven saying "This is My beloved Son, in whom I am well pleased."

Matt 3:16-17.

The Lord Jesus fore tells of the Spirit calling the Helper: Nevertheless I tell you the truth. It is to your advantage that I go away; for if I do not go away, the Healer will not come to you; if I depart, I will send Him to you.

John 16:7.

Again: However, when He, the Spirit of the truth; has come, He will guide you into all truth; for He will not speak on His own authority, but whatever He hears He will speak; and He will tell you things to come.

Matt 16:13.

In the Book of John it says: And I will pray the Father; and He will give you another Helper, that He may abide with you forever, the Spirit of truth, whom the world cannot receive, because it neither see Him nor knows Him, but you know Him, for He dwells with you and be in you.

John 14:16,17.

Prior He ascended into heaven; He give commandments to His apostles whom He had chosen; He commanded them not to depart from Jerusalem, but to wait for the Promise of the Father which He say you have heard from Me, for John truly baptized with water, but you shall be baptized with the Holy Spirit not many days from now......But you shall receive power when the Holy Spirit has come open you; and you shall be witnesses to Me in Jerusalem, and in all Judea and Samaria, and to the end of the earth.

Acts1:4-8.

Ten days after the ascension; When the Day of the Pentecost had fully come, they were all with one accord in one place. And suddenly there came a sound from heaven, as of a rushing mighty wind, and it filled the whole house where they were siting. Then there appeared to them divided tongues as of fire, and one sat upon each of them. And they were all filled with the Holy Spirit and began to speak with other tongues as the Spirit gave them utterance.

Acts 2:1-4.

It is a big difference in being guided by the Holy Spirit and being baptized in the Holy Spirit. The Lord Jesus before ascended, when He was with the disciple on earth He breathed on them to get the temporary power, and the same today the Holy Spirit move the heart help people to understand the Word of God give them faith to be able to repent of their sin but we need more then that we need to be baptized with the Holy Spirit to have the power to be witnesses. God give them the power through the baptism of the Holy Spirit on the day of the Pentecost with the speaking in tongue, and He give us today the same way after more than two thoU.S.nd years. All the Christians who believe and ask receive today the baptism of the Holy Spirit and they receive power from God to be witnesses to the end of the earth through the Gift of the Holy Spirit which poured through signs and wanders that accompany faith. God no opinion of what age, color, nationality or even religion that you are. Nor does God care to what church you go, or if you're rich or poor, or if you are male, or female, young, or old He is ready to give you the Holy Spirit if you believe. As long as you are ready to ask for it. There is no other greatest or joy on earth than it is to know that God is with you, and you fill his presence. He will be with you all your life if you let Him to be in control of your life.

The Answer

As for water baptism he is our covenant with God after repentance. It is the proof of our testimony before God and witnesses that we believe in Him, and that we agree to serve Him until our death. Usually it is made before receiving the baptism of the Holy Spirit but is not a rule and there are many who have received the Holy Spirit baptism before the water baptism. The water baptism is also called the baptism of repentance because is start with John the Baptist;

In those days John the Baptist came preaching in the wilderness of Judea telling everyone

"Repent, for the kingdom of heaven is at hand!" For this is he who was spoken of by the prophet Isaiah saying; The voice of one crying in the wilderness; Prepare the way of the Lord make His paths straight. Now John himself was clothed in camel's hair, with a leather belt around his waist; and his food was locust and wild honey. Then Jerusalem all Judea and all region around Jordan went out to him and were baptized by him in the Jordan, confessing their sin."

Mat 3:1-6.

The baptism don't save anyone but have something to do with our obedience of the Word of God because the baptism is the Lord commandment. The Scripture says: He who believes and is baptized will be saved; but he who does not believe will be condemned.

Mark 16:16.

The baptism also represent our death with Christ: knowing this, that our old man was crucified with Him that the body of sin might be done away with that we should no longer be slave of sin. For he who has died has been freed from sin. Now if we died with Christ we believe that we shall also live with Him. Rom 6:6-8, and resurrection with Him to a new life with good work pleasing God. The true Christians was baptize and we need to be baptized if we are Christians and want to obey the Word of God. There is no certain age to get the water baptism but need to be done when you know what you doing when you truly repent of dead works and by faith you want to serve the Lord who gave His life for you. This is our part and the Lord is doing His part and He will baptize you with the Holy Spirit. Lord Jesus help us to fulfill your will and prepare us through the Holy Spirit for your coming.

Amen!

"He who overcomes shall be clothed in white garments and I will not blot out his name from the Book of life, but I will confess his name before My Father and before His angels."

Rev 3:5

Chapter 4

Three Days and Three Nights

> "Now the Lord had said Abraham: Get out of your country, from your family and from your father's house, to a land that I will show you. I will make you a great nation, I will bless you and make your name great; and you shall be a blessing. I will bless those who bless you, and I will curse him who curses you; and in you all the families of the earth shall be blessed."
>
> Gen 12:1-4

Going to a prayer meetings like usually do, I had a revelation thru the Holy Spirit that the Lord ordained me to preach the Gospel. He has told me that I will help show the way of salvation over mountains, over the seas all the way to the end of the earth. At that moment I didn't understand what that mint, maybe because I was living in the communist time. During those days no one could leave the country. No one even dreamed about something like that because it was so impossible.

Next I was a member of a church with a very narrow path. Brothers were not allowed to wear a tie or even a watch on their arm. No one could have long hair, expensive clothing, jewelry, cars or tv. As for the women the sisters had to have their head covered, long sleeves. They also could not wear shoes with heels, rings, or necklaces. They could not wear makeup, or wear men's clothing. Another thing that could bring shame to you included to leave the country where he or she were born. So my question for myself was, "how could I dream of leaving the country?" I believed in every singe on of these rules.

There was even one time when I saw two brothers make a vow to the Lord. When they made this vow they completely cut their hair. After I witnessed this I went to go and cut my hair to humble myself before the Lord, but it did not last long. My wife didn't like me with hair that short and so I had leave my hair alone so that it may be capable of getting longer again. There was also another time where my wife had bought me a nice fur coat. She had said that she bought it for me to protect my back from the cold, or when I go to work on the bus. The only problem with the coat was that I couldn't take it to church, I was worried that my brothers may think that I was proud. I was ashamed to wear it until finally I sold it.

There were so many brothers from other churches who went west escaping from Romania but we don't know anybody from our church. A few years passed from the revelation and someone knocked on my door. I open the door and I saw a young man who introduced himself as Paul. Paul asked me if I am Constantin. After I assured him of my identity he invite me to go to a cafeteria to talk about some serious business. At first I was a bit worried because the communist regime have used several ways to get people, but the more I talked with Paul the more I realized that he is an honest man.

I went with him to the near cafeteria on the other side of the road from where I lived. I knew Paul had a problem, but I couldn't think of any way to bring the subject back to his issue, but in the end he told me that a friend of his gave him my name and the address. He said that he wanted to escape from Romania. He told me he was prepared for a long time. He had money he had his compass and everything else that he might have needed. The only problem was that he said he was afraid to go alone. He heard I am a man of faith and God will protect me and He will protect him to if he is coming with me. I saw him like an honest man. I did not suspect him to be from the communist party, and in my mind I was thinking can be sent from the Lord. I never thought to leave the country I could not believe that I can leave my family and go. Although my response was to only get rid of him I told him that this is a big decision, and that I will ask the Lord if is His will. If it is his will then we will met in three days Sunday in a specified place. I also told him if it is not the Lords will then then we wool never meet. After this we both agreed and he left.

After Paul left. Liter that afternoon I was feeling guilty for just telling Paul I was going to pray just to get rid of him, so I decided to actually go home and ask the Lord about I and Paul's conversation. I asked the Lord Three things all which were pretty much impossible to happen and I asked Him if it is His will I want all of this these to happen in three days. That is how I know it would be His will for me to go. I never told this to anyone not even my wife, but every day one of the prayer requests came to pass, and on the third day when the last request happened, I was frightened. I almost did not want to go, I would have to leave my family, my country, but I realized that actually it was God's will for me to go.

I remembered all the revelations I have had before about this. The third request was that the Lord prepare me the way out from the family overnight that way there was no suspicion from anyone. From the time my wife and I have gotten married we had never been separated. We were always together we lived together we were with each other every night, every day at work, we were always together, but this time something was coming up. My wife asked me if I could help my father-in-law with some business because he is not felling to well. So I needed to go to a little city to help them take care of his business. To do that I will be deeding to stay overnight and come home the next day.

After I take care of my father-in-law business on Sunday night, I will then meet with Paul and take the train and go to Stamora Moravita. Stamora Moravita is a valley very close to the border with Jugoslavia. After we got off from the train we got started to talk to some mine workers who drink outside of the store and if somebody saw us they will think we are with them. When night came we went out of town and stayed in a bus station with some people. An officer even came by but a small car drove by and stole their attention. In that moment we fled the area before an officer could see us. We ran a quickly as possible to the fence.

As soon as our hands grasped upon the wire we started to climb hoping that no one would see us. After we jumped over the fence it was dark and we heard the dogs barking, waning the officers that someone had wrongfully passed through. Our emotions were full of concern just from hearing the soldiers, dogs and officers behind us. We then head toward one trench with thorns it made it even more difficult to run away from them. It was so difficult that Paul left some of his things there in the trenches, he wanted to be sure if they caught us that they wouldn't think that we were trying to leave the country permanently with all of our belongings.

We stayed there a few hour of the night until we realized that we were near a military unit by the border. When we try to come out from the trench we hear the solders shout, stop, stop or I shoot, hands up, I was very scared at first but soon we realized that they only say that to scare people. We come out from the trench and jump up from one tree to another until we get behind of the military unit. There was a hill with a new plantation tree across and we need to climb in elbows and knees climbing the stairs so we couldn't be seen from any military personnel. When we reached the summit I came across a cornfield and we entered in it be able to stand up and walk normally because we are protected by the field and nobody can see us now. We passed the cornfield with God's help but we did not find the border in the first night.

And because it was morning already we looked around to find a good place to hide and rest to be ready for the next night to cross the border. We descended into a valley which had lots of bushes with thorns and around a big green grass which in September get lot of water overnight. We manage to get inside for protection but we were soaked wet, hunger and cold. We seat down on the ground back to back to warm each other up. Once we were both dry and warmed up we immediately fell asleep. Later on the day the shepherds come with the sheep to gather them in the area. As they shepherds were doing that there was a fox being chased by dogs, so the fox came to hide inside the same space he had claimed. We asked the Lord to protect us and not let the dogs smell us. When I opened my eyes I saw two pieces of quince in a tree by us and after we praised God we brought them down we prepared to eat to give us strength. We stayed there until it was evening and all the workers and the shepherds got home.

Once we were certain there was no one in sight we slowly came out from hiding walked away. The compass then pointed us to a direction we were not prepared for, a forest. Once we walked through the forest it became so dark that you could not see anything. Because of the blinding darkness we were walking into branches. So because we were not able to see we decided to go another rout. I heard a sound of the water leak and once we came out. Now we tried to walk on the side of the forest. We didn't get too far until we find an old road that seemed like it hadn't been used for a long time. But besides the fact of the age, the road looked like it was going in the exact direction of our destination.

We walk on it for few hours until we found an old military post. We walked by it with emotions and once we passed the forest we were able to see a light. As we got closer to the right we realized that there is another military place there. These soldiers also used a very bright light which they move around to control the area. Then once again we found ourselves jumping from tree to tree, to prevent ourselves from getting caught. We did this until we knew the light was out. Once we got through the lighted arena we found a sugar beet garden. We took some for the road. Not too much time had passed until we reached the next morning, and because we had not yet reached the boarder, we had decided to find another location to rest and hide until the sun had fallen, and it was safer to go to our next destination.

We then discovered a corn farm on one side of the field had been tended to while the other half had not even been touched. They cut the body and put them together and make them like a Indian style house to protect them for rain until they are ready to take them home. We decide to go on the side of the road where the corn is already picked up thinking that it was possible they the farmers could return at any moment of time to gather and cut the remaining corn. We didn't want to risk getting caught over corn so we picked one of the "corn houses" up and take it to another nearby location so that we can rest.

We fell asleep extremely fast that night, the corn actually helped keep the heat within its little hut, so it made it a lot easier to fall asleep. Soon the sun rose and we heard the tractor coming with a lot of people talking. They came to pick up the corn on the left side of the road. Thank God we did not get caught! They came down and put their food and water on our side of the road inside the corn body house. Each person took a row, there was enough each to take a corn house and put them on the tractor bed, then return for more.

From time to time they take a little break, they would come to our side of the road where they put their food and they would eat, drink, and go back to work. You can imagine how we were capable of staying there one whole day and only a few feet away from them. There were times where the men would get even closer near our corn house just so they could get away from the other farmers so they could use the restroom. Oh and there was also some mice coming to eat the corn from the corn house and would come inside. We couldn't scream nor stand up because we didn't want to get caught. After they finish the job and put all the corn on the tractor they come take their stuff put it all on the tractor and leave.

Finally when people left we went out again and started walking. We were so excited, that we couldn't believe that we were about to reach the boarder soon. We walk very fast and determined through the land. Through the pastures we passed a cemetery close to a city where we found only two big nuts to eat. And again we reached another morning and don't find the boarder. We heard a bell ring, from a cow or a ship we did not know but apparently it was near a village. Although we could not see anything. It was early in the morning with very thick fog. As we were walking we saw wire bales of straw on the ground and we thought that it would be a good idea to build a shelter with them like a little house to take a rest until the evening time. I put two bales on each side two on the back two on the top, I broke one and put on the ground like a mattress. We went inside and pulled one in the front of us and we fell asleep like a baby. I don't know how long I slept, but when we heard the cow bells we got up. We looked outside there was still fog. It was probably around ten o'clock in the morning, don't know, but I didn't have the patience to the evening. So I broke the house and started to walk to the border.

Looking down on the ground we saw lots of ripe blackberry which I never saw before. The berries were very sweet. We took them by the hand and stated eating, we didn't even care about the thorns. We poked our self so much I didn't fill the thorns pain any more. As we are walking and eating blackberry we don't pay too much attention, the fog is almost gone and when I lifted my eyes could not believe what I saw. We are near the military unit we are in the middle of land with nothing around us to hide this time. In front of us only thirty feet a high military post a solder with one arm was walking around to see the area.

We saw wired fence protecting they're corn fields. In front of us was only a few feet. Now we didn't feel any emotion at all and decide to go in the corn field in their garden. We walked normally, and when we reached the fence I picked up the wire to help Paul go in and after that he pick up the wire and I went through. We saw again how God protected us. We both knew that He closed the eyes of the soldier to not be able to see us. Praise God!

We stayed there for few minute to see if is something happened and when we noticed that everything was quiet we tried to take advantage of the little wind. When the wind blew and moved the corn we walked a few rows further. Once the wind settled we made sure not to walk any further so that the soldier couldn't detect our movement within the corn fields. Within the fields of corn were many roads which went into several different directions. After walking farther through the corn rows we realized that we were on the end of the field. All of a sudden I had this feeling that the border was right on the other side of the bushes ahead of us. After we were hit with excitement, we decided to wait for the sun to go down. We believed that it would be easier to escape the border line if the soldier's vision was blocked by the night.

After few minutes we heard soldiers approaching very closely with their dogs. We thought we were caught for sure, although we noticed that they were only switching shifts with other soldiers for the night. They walked so close to us that we overheard their conversation about Craiova University soccer team. Praise God again they don't smell us! We stopped and held our breath for as long as we possibly could. Once they passed us by we finally released our breath with praise. Soon when the sun went down we managed to go crawl on our bellies slowly through the remaining distance through the bushes. As soon as we fully made it through we made a sudden pause. We wanted to make sure that there was no security preventing us to cross. Once the path was clear we finally we made it through the boarder and entered in to Jugoslavia.

Three nights, it took us three nights to get where we were and now I figured out why it had taken us so long to cross over... The reason was because we had walked parallel to the boarder rather than walking straight through. So instead of making it through the boarder within one night we spent two more days and nights trying to cross.

It was so difficult for me to leave my country, I had lived there all my life, it was the place I was born, the place were all my family was. Many would talk about leaving but as I said before we as Romanians could not do it, but with God everything is possible. When He calls for someone to do His will He has His own form of plans. First He changes their heart, He will then give them the strength and power to do His will. On the pages of the Scripture we find people who have done this and I will like to think of one of them Abraham. We could al learn from him learn something from him.

The Obedience

"Now the Lord had said to Abram; "Get out from your country from your family and from your father house to a land that I will show you. I will make you a great nation; I will bless you and make your name great; and you shall be a blessing. I will bless those who bless you, and I will curse him who curses you and in all the families of the earth shall be blessed."

Gen 12:1-4.

Abraham was one of the important figure of the Old Testament the Jewish traces their family tree from Abram. One time when he was living with his wife Sarah and his father in

Haran, Abram receive a message from God to leave his country and go to another country. God don't tell him what country he need to go to but he need to be obedient to God's voice and need to walk with the Lord. Abram was obedient to the Lord and accepted without more information even he was old maybe for around 75 years. We see how God can call people for his mission at any age. Was a call for Abraham to believe in God even his promise about a child was not full filled yet, the country he is going to was filled with people with different cultures, they have no resources, no children but Abram needed to trust the Lord not in himself.

This is our problem today we need to learn from Abraham we need to believe in God not in our talents or ability. I believe this was a call for transformation to learn to depend on God. Abraham journey at first was to have some profit for him and his family but was the other way around. Was a call to hold nothing also but only to the Lord. Instead to hold something for himself he lived the rest of his life to learn to give and to lose. The reason was to see that you don't need anything else only the Lord. This is an encouragement to obey the Lord completely and walk with Him by faith. To try to do what you can is not enough that happens with some of us, we only try to do what he asks of us rather than actually doing it. If you want to answer to the call of God you need the transformation your life through the Holy Spirit.

Yes many peoples try to go to church every Sunday read the Bible to pray to give the ten percent to the Lord thinking was good enough but not one of them make you holy, only God can give you the courage only He has power to change your life. We hear about God people like: Abraham, Jacob, Moses, Solomon, Samson, Peter, Paul what they have in common? They gave to the

Lord everything they had in their life: their passion, their pride, their gift, their plans, their agenda, their heart, mind, and soul. To get your right you need to put everything in Gods hand. If we look at Abraham he started when his father finished in Haran the same us we need to continue what God start with our fathers in local church or in mission field.

One of the good thinks Abraham did, he built an altar in every place he have a revelation from God. Another thing we learn from the life of Abraham, God did not call Abraham only for his benefit, but God is looking more for His benefit for His peoples and for theirs future that is God passions.

"A man's heart plans his way, but the Lord directs his steps."

Prov 16:9.

"For I know the thoughts that I think toward you, says the Lord, thoughts of peace and not evil, to give you a future and a hope."

Jer 29:11.

God help us to learn the lesson to be completely obedient to the Lord for the rest of our life.

Amen!

"To him who overcomes I will give to eat from the tree of life, which is in the midst of the Paradise of God."

Rev 2:7

Chapter 5

Fifteen Days Without the Bible

"But the Lord was with Joseph and showed him
mercy, and He gave him favor in the sight of the keeper
of the prison. And the keeper of the prison committed to
Joseph's hand all the prisoners who were in the prison;
whatever they did there, it was his doing. The keeper of
the prison did not look into anything that was under
Joseph's authority, because the Lord was with him and
whatever he did, the Lord made it prosper."

Gen 39:21-23.

After we crossed the border into Yugoslavia we look for some
evidence to be sure we pass the border because the strip we
crossed was not the way we imagined. It was one very nice strip
of sand. Here the grass was different, the corn was higher and
thicker like a tree, and had more stalks on them. Between the
rows a large and dense grass and was very hard to walk through.
After a while we got the smell of grapes and we went by smell
until I found a vineyard, we sat down and ate as much we could,
after that we took off our jackets tied the sleeves together and
put more grape to have on the road. Going further into the new

land we came to a village. The people don't lay down, we heard they speaking and we go near to hear the language they speak and we understood that they were speaking Serbian. We found bags of fertilizer near that village and even the writing was in the Serbian language. We also found an electric power post with a dead skull which was different then in Romania. We believed we were in Yugoslavia.

Because we were so tired we looked around for a place to rest. After a few hours we found a field of corn stalk made like Indian houses to protect them from rain by the road. So like we did before we decided to make one large home to stay inside to go in and rest. I don't know how much we slept but we were awaken by the sound of cars. We cleaned our clothes and went to the road to take our chance to go to Italy. I made signs with my hand to try and get us a ride from the cars passing by, but no one stopped. Finally a bus had stopped, as they opened their door we realized that we just asked one of the buses who take more soldiers to different locations. As we stood outside the bus two officers stepped down the stairs. The officers then asked us for our papers. Unfortunately this is how they found out that we had just escaped from Romania. The soldiers then decided they were going to take us to the police office in Virset.

After the security office had checked us they notified us that because we pass their border they are obliged to punish us with fifteen days in jail. The only good part about this whole delay, was that they agreed to take us where we wanted to migrate. After we have paid off our time in jail for 15 days they took us to the Virset jail. While we were there they took our belongings from us. Things such as my Bible, and my hymn song book. They told us not to worry, and that they promised to return all of our things after our timed punishment. They showed us our cell where we were going to be sleeping, where we would eat, and they also explained all the rules of the jail. They also assured us if we ever became board that they would allow us to go and work in the city. There was no obligation for us to work, but at least we were given options.

I had decided to go out and work every day until we were released to the lumber company. Our boss was very nice, on some occasions the people who bought our lumber would leave tips, with these tips we would return to our boss. Our boss had agreed that whenever we accumulated money from our buyers he would use that money to buy us workers our necessities from the town. I felt so blessed and protected inside and out, praise God! We thought that if at the end of our fifteen days that we will ask the soldiers to take us to Italy, Germany, or Austria to emigrate into the U.S. But the Serbs who were in prison they told us that we still do not know for sure it is the risk to give us back to Romania because the president of Romania Ceausescu from time to time make some trade with Yugoslavia he give them salt and the Serbs give them back the prisoners. They also tell us to know when they release us if the officer come dressed in military clothes and if they put us handcuffs on our hand and take us to the police office in the city and see some body wash the car they will take you to Romania so that they might receive a good impression on the border. But if they come dressed casual, they don't use the handcuffs, and they don't wash their car, then there is no danger. With all of that being said there was a chance to stay in Yugoslavia or to go elsewhere where they help immigrate people.

When our turn came for me and Paul to get free, they called us by name and give us back all our belonging, two officer dress in military costume waiting for us. They put the handcuffs on us and took us to the police car. There they put us in a little room under the stairs and locked us up. We understood that we needed to wait there. The room had a little window, with metal bars and on the walls around were bits of writing from the other people who had been here once before. Everyone had engraved their names and the date they were being sent back to Romania .We helped each other to get up to look out on the window where we saw the police court. We were able to see the soldiers washing the car that they brought us in. This whole experience reminded us what we were told in jail. Everything they had mentioned was happening, and our chances returning to Romania grew larger than we wanted.

Paul suddenly became very scared, he then began trying to hide some money he had left over from tips in some old shoes. He took the shoes and hid them in a garbage bag in a corner. He said he had done this, just in case they do find us, that their punishment wouldn't be as terrible. Paul then pulled the belt from his pants to try and hang himself. He pleaded that he did not want to suffer the consistent beatings in the Romanian jail. He said that he would rather die now than suffer through pure torcher. I prayed to God to have mercy on us. I begged Paul not to lose faith in God. I told him we must stay strong, and trust in him that he will continue to bless us. Paul then decided to return the money back into his pocket. I don't know how long we stayed there until the two officers come back to release us from the cell. They talked very nicely with us as if nothing had happened. We were invited in the car without handcuffs. They noticed how afraid we were and tried to reassure us that we were on our way to Belgrad.

Now because we worked in town for fifteen days we learned the roads and we know after few kilometers the main road split.

One road went to Belgrad and goes to Romania. We couldn't speak, all we could do was shed tears of fear. With one hand holding Paul's hand and the other holding the seat, we looked straight ahead to see in what direction we were going. I pray to God and I saw Paul is ready to do something if the car is heading to Romania to jump to the driver or open the door and jump outside. We waited at the intersection with nervousness, and when I saw it I was not able to seat we are in air and we saw the car is headed to Romania and as Paul was preparing to take the driver and expect me to do the same, in just a few seconds the car entered to the gas station on the corner and the officer realized again that we are scare and they tell us they put gas and going straight to the refugee camp near Belgrad.

I don't know if this officer's play with us intentionally to scare us or they jest take Romanian road to turn on the gas station on the right and go straight to Belgrad. This was one of the most nerve racking moments of my life. We both were exhausted and weak. We couldn't talk for several hours out of shock. They took us to a temporary refuge camp in near Belgrad where they hold refuges from all the communist countries. There in one room they hold over fifty people, who were asleep on the bed. Half of the room had mattresses, the other half slept on tables. This was a real jail, we don't know how long we would stay there or what they would do with us. Here in the camp they take us out of the room only to eat. We are always in a line. Inside the camp even more disturbing, toilet was completely exposed, and there wasn't even a place to shower. The place was constantly smelling of urine and sweat. In the camps we were exposed to things that we had never seen nor heard ever before. There was different types of people in the camp. There were gangsters from Bucharest, they would always be telling everyone what they had done without fear.

The gangsters would always look around the room to see if they could find one new to pick on. One day they saw me I read the Bible and confessed the Word of God to an old man who slept beside me on the table. I was so blessed and thankful that here they allowed me to have my Bible. The Gangsters had called out my name putting me on a common carpet where they bully and beat others daily. They called me and put me on the carpet like usual, some body try to condemn me and make me to renounce my faith in Jesus. They said if I didn't that they will condemn me to death. I expected them to pull the carpet and beat me up very hard, before I said anything I was praying in my mind. One of a sudden one of them stood up who had authority over all of them and commanded them to let me go. Without any questions asked they let me go and took somebody else.

I was surprised and didn't understand why their lead let me go. Later I had the opportunity to talk to the person who saved me and found out the truth. He told me he was a very bad person in his life and he had done many bad things. For all these crimes he had committed while he was in Romania he had been put in jail. While he was in jail, his wife had repented and asked to receive Jesus in her life and started to go to church. When he got out from jail he beat her because she no longer go out with him to have fun. All she wanted to do was to go to church, then he beat her and not allow her go to church out of jealousy. He knew she don't do anything wrong, but he don't have the power to accept this true. He continued to still beat her. Although no matter how many times that he beat her she continued to pray for him. Finally he left the country. When these guys took me on the carpet and try to condemn me he saw his wife wrongfully condemned by him and he cannot see that and old them to let me go. He remembered the innocence of his wife and he was sorry for me and let me go free. I thanked him for what he did for me. I try to comfort him and tell him to try and contact his wife when he had a spare chance. Finally, after fifteen days of nervousness, not knowing if the soldier were going to take you back to Romania. For those many days we lived in the misery of the awful scent of urine and sweat, we lived in the risk of one day can being beaten by gangsters. We lived and slept through the uncomfortable places to rest.

One night they open the big metal door and called us by our name and asked us to board a bus and told us that they were going to take us to Italy. I sat on the first bench behind the driver to be able to see the road better. I was so happy to find my seat near the front of the bus. Seating in front of me was a Brother named Stefan. He too was from Romania. He told me he was in a new building that was near ours. He said that he had seen me a few times whenever we were all in line to eat in the cafeteria. I was thankful that Stefan was there to accompany me on the rest of my trip, he made the trip to Italy so much more enjoyable with him to talk to. After the bus left Belgrad and took the highway to Italy. When you hear about someone that is in jail, or that someone would had once been to jail you are automatically begin thinking did that person do to get there? Not all who go to jail are criminals nor are they guilty of being a bad person. It is true that the government's system has made so many mistakes. Hopefully the innocent are capable of being released from the prisons and jails soon.

The Instrument Used

So I find an example in Genesis 37, that Joseph which was one of the youngest children of Jacob after BeniAmen. His father Jacob love him very much because he have him on old age which attracted hate of his brothers. Joseph was endowed by God with a gift of dreams and one day when he confess the dream to his brothers they become upset and say he is proud and they took him and sold him to a caravan that went to Egypt. Joseph flourished in Egypt and became the man of the master trust worthy until one day he was falsely accused and was thrown into prison. God allow some to get in jail to learn a lesson that cannot learn elsewhere that was happened with Joseph. He had a great challenge; He was treated very badly from his brothers, he was sold and became a slave in a foreign country, he was falsely accused and put in jail. In the midst of all the problem he remained patient and faithful to God. Even that somebody may forget, but God did not forget and now we can learn some lessons from the life of Joseph. We all in our life go to various tests and some even to jail.

"These things I have spoken to you, that in Me you may have peace, in the world you will have tribulation; but be of good cheer, I have overcome the world."

John 16:33.

"For I am persuaded that neither death nor life, nor angels nor principalities nor powers, not things present nor things to come, nor height nor death, nor any other created thing, shall be able to separate us from the love of God which is in Christ Jesus our Lord."

Rom 8:38-39.

Duty of Joseph in jail. Gen 40:1-4. God allowed that after some complains, the king of Egypt put in jail his cupbearer and his baker under the supervision of Joseph. This was not happen by accident in God is no accidents is only an appointed time. God brought Joseph face to face with the man who later will help him to be released from jail. So in our life always have to be very careful with whom we meet because God can bring them in our life to test us or to bring a purpose to our life and trying to direct our steps.

"A man's heart plans his way, but the Lord direct his steps."

Prov 16:9.

And while they were in jail one morning Joseph see them they are sad and ask them, why your face is dull today? They replied, we dreamed a dream and there is no one to interpret it. Joseph tell them the interpretation come from God and let me know your dreams. (Gen 40:7-8.)

And they start to tell Joseph their dreams, and Joseph give them the interpretation to the cup bearer said that in three days you will be taken out of prison and be put back in the Pharaoh service, but after you will be released to remember about him and tell Pharaoh that he was put in jail unfairly and help him to be released. And also Joseph tell the baker that in three days he will be executed. And just as Joseph say happened after three days the butler was released and put back in service of Pharaoh and the baker was hanged, but the butler forgot about Joseph. We notice here that Joseph had the gift of dreams and the interpretation of the dreams and after his dreams he was sold in Egypt but he continued and stay firm in the Lord and even in prison he is in control. No matter what we get in life or where we come to believe that he wanted God an believe that it is actually working for our good and for those with whom we come in contact even if we do not see but we will understand after it.

The Scripture says: "And we know that all things work together for good to those who love God to those who are called according to His purpose."

Rom 8:28.

After the butler was release from jail Joseph expected to get some news from him but he forgot about him and the injustice maid to him and pass two more years. Maybe Joseph was grieved at this time but again the word tell us not to put our trust in people that actually help come from the Lord:

"I will lift up my eyes to the hills from whence comes my help? My help comes from the Lord who made heaven and earth."

Ps 121:1.

Joseph learn that God's unseen hand preparing everything for us and is never too late or too early for us He is always in time. Even if we are in prison of suffering from or what or what might be, or even in prison unjustly and we are discouraged, it is hard to see you leave though, but we know we are not forgotten or abandoned by God and in His time, He will visit us and make us free.

What was the difference between Joseph and others who were in prison with him? He always know that the Lord is with him:

"The keeper of the prison did not look into anything that was under Joseph's authority, because the Lord was with him, and whatever he did the Lord made him prosper."

Gen 39:23.

After two years Pharaoh had two dreams and he was mad because no one in his kingdom was able to interpret his dreams. The butler now remembered Joseph when he was in prison he have a dream and Joseph give him the interpretation exactly and told Pharaoh about the mistake he made and about Joseph. Then the King commanded to release Joseph from prison because nobody can interpret his dream and bring him to the king. After Pharaoh tell Joseph the dreams he have with the seven fat cows and seven ugly and gaunt which eat up the seven fine looking and fat cows, and also the second dream with seven heads of grain and seven thin heads which devoured the seven plumb and full heads. God give Joseph the interpretation of the dreams and tell pharaoh that will be seven years of plenty followed by seven years of poverty over the land of Egypt, and tell pharaoh what he need to do. Because pharaoh like the wisdom of Joseph he say to Joseph:

"Because God make you know all of these things there is none to be as skillful and wise as you. You shall be over my house and all my people will obey your commandments, only my throne will rise above of you. Hire I give you the all country of Egypt."

Gen 41:39-41.

63

God caused Joseph to be released at the time appointed by Him and his faith and patience was paid because behind them came to be used of God in Egypt and he was a blessing for his family and was able to save his father and his brothers from the fAmene in the land of Canaan and they were protected in the land of Egypt. Therefore my beloved don't be disappointed if you suffer, you need to know God know everything. He knows you by name, trusts in Him and He will deliver you, but until then be a light, work with the gift God gave to you, now is just preparation for the blessing that will come upon you and your family. Lord give us patience.

Amen!

"He who overcomes shall not be hurt by the second death."

Rev 2:11

Chapter 6

Christian to Freedom

But Daniel purposed in his heart that he would not defile himself with the portion of the King's delicacies, nor with the wine which he drank; therefore he requested of the chief of the eunuchs that he might not defile himself. Now God had brought Daniel into the favor and the good will of the chief of the eunuchs. And the chief of the eunuchs said to Daniel. I fear my lord the king, who has appointed your food and drink. For why should he see your faces looking worse than the young men who are your age? Then you would endanger my head before the king. So Daniel said to the steward whom the chief of the eunuchs had set over Daniel, Hananiah, Mishel, and Azariah. Please test your servants for ten days, and let them give us vegetables to eat and water to drink. Then let our appearance be exAmened before you, and the appearance of the young man who eat the portion of the king's delicacies; and as you see fit, so deal with your servants. So he consented with them in this matter, and tested them for ten days. And the end of ten days their features appeared better and fatter in flesh than all the young men who ate the portion of the king's delicacies.

Dan 1:8-15.

We went all night with the bus from Belgrade and in the morning we reached the border with Italy at Trieste and I was exhausted. There the bus dropped some of us off then returned on the road. They drove by the border and maybe around noon time they stopped the bus again at a military post on the border with Italy. Here is where they brought everyone off the bus. They took us two by two and put us in very small rooms with metals door like in jail and tell us to wait. You wouldn't believe the amount of people who suffered and lost the patience. They were beating with their fists and kicking the metal doors to make a big noise. No one knew what would happen next. Later on the soldiers brought us something to eat. During the evening only a few people were allowed to be taken out of the cell. When our turn came they took me and Paul in a small car. When we got in the car they drove us few kilometers up the forest on the border. We expected them to lead us to the Italian authority on the border or to take us to the first town to deliver us to the police office, or to the immigration camp, but was nothing like this. The car stop in the middle of the night on the forest hill. The driver was a nice man, he left us and try to tell us few things, and then went a little further and showed us some foot concrete pillars on the ground. He told us this is the border with Italy. He also showed some lights from a city in Italy he embraced us and wished us a good journey, and to our amazement he let us go and cross the border into Italy the same way we crossed from Romania in Yugoslavia. He got in the car and left and we started walking in the forest towards the lights of the first city from Italy.

After more than a month we were free to walk again, this time in Italy where I really wanted to go. We walked all night but this time we were very happy, and look like we flying. In the morning we reached the city Molfalcone. There we are we began looking for the police station to ask them to help us to find an Immigration camp to immigrate to the U.S. With God's help we found the police station and on the intercom they told us that we were too early, and that we need to wait outside until they opened. Once opened we are welcomed inside where he talked with us by the translator and told us to have a little patience and they will take us to the train station. They also said that they will give us tickets and send us to Roma. There we will continue on with the bus stop to an immigration camp in Latina. There at the camp they will assist us with the necessary documents for immigrate to get to the U.S. Now the time passed quickly and we were told as soon as someone came. They took us to the train station to buy the ticket for us and put us on a train heading to Rome. I could feel the air of freedom again. It was so nice to be free, I felt like I was in another world. The people were better, everything was different. It was so nice in train, I no longer wanted to stop, but after few hours we reached the most famous city of Rome. The capital of the earth. We were not even tired we had so much energy and wanted to look around and see everything. It was so wonderful, we looked for the bus station and praised God it was not far. The bus station was just behind the train station. We took the bus to the city of Latina.

After we reach Latina we asked for the immigration camp. They gave us some directions to the location and direction we needed to go. Once we found the place we needed to go, we ended up having to wait once again because it was too early to open the office. When the office opened we spoke with a translator. I filled out the politic asylum to immigrate to U.S. Soon after the application was completed they told us the camp rules. They tell us where we will be staying where we eat, then told us that we have to wait patiently for the announcement when we have to present to the interview with the consul of the American Embassy in Rome. They will be the ones who decide our case. The camp had several simple buildings like an army unit. They had rooms on both sides, and in the middle of the halls were open bathrooms. There were open bathrooms on one side and a lavatory on the other. There I was staying with three other men. There were four to a room and I was happy because all where Christian and we all got along very well. The camp entrance was guarded by Italian police, but the people inside were free individual and not enslaved in any way. They did so many things, that many might have been scared about.

I learned that the people went to the gate early in the morning where the Italian patrons drive by and took people who were in need of jobs. I was also in various places, one day when I was able to help a family with their construction needs, I was grateful that God give me favor and allowed me to work there with the family until I was immigrated into the U.S. They were a wonderful family because they treated me as family. I ate with them on the table every day for more than seven months. It was a blessing for me as I was able to get some money and help my family from Romania which I send several packages. Every day when I come back to Camp I checked the list which was the place at the entrance of the camp.

On the weekend with other friends went to Rome and visited the Coliseum where Christians were thrown to be torn by the wild beast in the arena. Another time I went to visit the jail where Peter and Paul were imprisoned. Another time I was to the catacombs which were some underground tunnels used by Christian in secret when they were persecuted for their faith in Jesus by the romans. All of these places were only but stories to me that I heard people speaking about it but now by the grace of God I was able to see them with my own eyes. This strengthened my faith, I remember everything what the Christians suffered for. Their faith made encouraged the future generations strength to grow stronger in the Lord. On my journey I also visited Vatican St. Peter Catholic Church. This church was a true masterpieces of art, it was just like a museum. I also visited several places in Rome like this, and on every intersection of roads is a center with beautiful fountains and statues. I never became tired from looking around. thousands of visitors who walked the streets of Rome would be taking photos or making movies of how the Europeans lived their lives here in Rome. I visited Naples, where I saw the biggest and the most beautiful boat in my life. The boat had several floors with balconies that were crafted in such a way that I cannot explain, they just seemed beautiful.

Finally after three months I was called to the American Embassy in Rome for an interview. They asked me how I was persecuted for my faith about my family about the military service if I was a party member and why I want to emigrate in U.S. I answered all the question and I tell them the truth, when I was a young man before the army where I was working the supervisor told me if I accept to became party member I will have an easy military service. He convinced me but after I came from the military service I repented and received Jesus in my heart and in the company I work for, they make a conference. Here is where they first tried to convince me to renounce my faith, and because I told them I refused to renounce they kicked me out of the party saying that I was traitor.

When the interview came to a close they told me that they will announce me, and I later then returned to Latina in camp. I still didn't know if I was approved or not. I had overheard some people say that a few people who went into the interview after I had left my interview were able to leave the camp before me. However I remained faithful to God I went to church camp or go to the Latina church and during the week we gathered in prayer. We gathered either in our room or in a family some brothers and witness's. I remained faithful with what God promised. I knew he would pull through with what He wanted me to accomplish. Here with so much freedom you can see the true Christians, it was not easy to stay in holiness when there when there is so much temptation to perform a sin surrounding you.

It was always very dangerous to go out at night time, even with the police being out on the street, bad things continued to happen. The police only stood at the entrance doors, but you see all the bad things happened within the camp. Once someone was inside the camp they could do whatever they wanted to do. For example one time there was practically a revolution going on between the Romanians and Albanians. It went so far that they all began to kill each other. From time to time the people even formed some hunger strike to get the attention of the United Nations to get the immigration faster.

With all of these things going on I found the way to relax. I would sometimes take my bike and go to the Mediterian Sea. As I came to the sea I would walk on the sand for hours, and listen to the water. It was so wonderful to hear the waves and the birds singing. One time to pass the time faster I got the cleaning job on camp that a friend had once recommended. This job took place early in the morning. After I finished the job for the day

I would find something to eat before I was needed to go to my next job in Latina. In all of this time I am glad that the Lord called me to this test of faith. I thank God that He strengthened me and helped me to remain faithful to Him. After almost eight months I found my name on the list to immigrate in U.S. Praise God! After I had seen so many Christians who had so much freedom, all I saw them focus on was money and pleasures instead of holiness and faith in God, I was thinking about the young Daniel.

The Holiness

In the time of Jehoiakim king of Judah, Nebuchadnezzar king of the Babylon came against Jerusalem and conquered it and took from Judah part of the vessels of God house and some young handsome man without blemish wisely was to be trained to serve Nebuchadnezzar in his house. They were given many riches and the emperor has ordained with what they eat every day. They needed to be fed from the king's food, and from his wine to keep them up for three years and after that he would be put in the Kings house to serve him. Among them was them was Daniel, Hananiah, Mishael, and Azariah and the chief of the eunuchs gave them a different names, Beltshazzar, Shadrach,Meshach, and Abednego. Daniel decided not to defile himself with the king food and wine and ask the chief eunuchs not to compel to be defiled. Dan 1:8.The chief eunuchs feared the king but God changed his heart and let Daniel and his friends for ten days eat only vegetables. Only then did the king see the difference between them and other young man which eat the king food. After the ten days they were better at the face and they are fatter than all young man who eat from king table. When the time came they were put in the king service.

God allowed the young men, who didn't have much experience with God, and they were about 15 or 16 years old, and already there taken captive with no family, to be put through God's test. What you would you do if you were in Daniel place? Would you have the courage to stand for your faith or you have hidden in your heart saying, I'm not repented, or I'm not baptized, I'm far from home from my parents, or would you say something like I have time to repent there is nothing wrong from eating the kings food, I can do what others young man do... I don't want to be embarrassed with my friends. But Daniel resolved not to defile himself. Someone said, "A holy life is one that has been set aside for God."

> "Pure and undefiled religion before God the Father is this; to visit orphans and widows in their trouble and to keep oneself unspotted from the world."
>
> James 1:27.

Do not defile yourself: mind, body and soul.

A) Daniel took the decision not to defile his mind, in other words a filthy mind will dictate how to live. The Book of Joshua it is said: "The book of the Law shall not depart from your mouth, but you shall meditate in it day and night, that you may observe to do according to all that is written in it. For then you will make your way prosperous, and then you will have good success." Joshua 1:8. Meditate on the Word of God and not be defiled.

B) Daniel resolved not to defiled his body with the food and wine from the king table because he never eat the food offered to idols.

"And do not present your members as instruments of unrighteousness to sin, but present yourselves to God as being alive from the dead, and your members as instruments of righteousness to God."

Rom 6:13.

With his mind already made up to God in holiness was easier to control his heart and body and become a light in the midst of darkness.

"Therefore come out from among them and be separate, say the Lord. Do not touch what is unclean, and I will receive you, I will be a Father to you, and you shall be my sons and daughters, says the Lord Almighty."

2 Cor 6:17-18.

C) Daniel resolved not to defile his soul. Daniel stood for what was right and his testimony and receive favor in the eyes of the chief of eunuchs.

"When a man's ways please the Lord, He makes even his enemies to be at peace with him."

Prov 16:7.

Daniel has put his faith in God, more important than human judgment.

"And do not fear those who kill the body but cannot kill the soul. But rather fear Him who is able to destroy both soul and body in hell."

Matt 10:28.

Daniel and his three friends took a good decisions not to defile themselves with the food and wine from the king's table which has loved by God and make them receive fever in the eyes of the king which receive them in his house and put them in his service. How good would it be if we do the same, to take decision to do not defile with the things in this world and live in holiness in body soul and spirit to be ready for the King of Kings and Lord of Lords who is ready to put us in His service. God help us.

Amen!

"Because you have kept My command to persevere, I also will keep you from the hour of trial which shall come upon the whole world, to test those who dwell on the earth."

Rev 3:10

Chapter 7

Crossing the Jordan

"And Joshua said, By this you shall know that the living God is among you, and that He will without fail drive out from before you the Canaanites and the Hittites and the Hivites and the Perizzites and the Ghirgashites and the Amorites and the Jebusites; Behold, the ark of the covenant of the Lord, of all the earth is crossing over before you into the Jordan. Now therefore, take for yourselves twelve man from the tribes of Israel, one man from every tribe. And it shall come to pass, as soon as the soles of the feet of the priest who bear the ark of the Lord, the Lord of all the earth, shall rest in the waters of the Jordan that the waters that come down from upstream, and they shall stand as a heap. So it was, when the people set out from their camp to cross over the Jordan, with the priests bearing the ark of the covenant before the people and as those who bore the ark came to the Jordan, and the feet of the priests who bore the ark dipped in the edge of the water for (the Jordan overflows all its banks during the whole time of harvest) that the waters which came down from the upstream stood still, and rose in a heap very far away at Adam, the city that is beside Zaretan. So the waters that went down into the Sea of the Arabah, the Salt Sea, failed, and were cut off, and the people crossed over opposite Jericho. Then the priests who bore the ark of the covenant of the Lord stood firm on the ground in the midst of the Jordan; and all Israel crossed over on dry ground, until all the people had crossed completely over the Jordan."

Josh 3:10-17

When I was called to immigration in U.S. they took us by a bus to the airport, from there they put us on a plane to New York. There was probably over three hundred people leaving to the U.S. This was the first time I saw an airplane so big. It was a lovely flight, in fact it was one of the greater days of my life. First because I was full filling the prophecies to go to America, the greatest country on earth which is a refuge place for all the persecuted Christian from all over the earth. Praise God for this wonderful place! Secondly because it was the first time I ever flew on a plane and while being so high up in the clouds, I feel as though I am close to heaven. It was the longest day of my life as well. I left Rome on noon time and arrive in New York on evening with few hours difference. I remembered when Joshua commanded the sun to stop in the sky until he retaliated on his enemies.

"So the sun stood still, and the moon stopped, till the people had revenge upon their enemies"

Josh 10:13.

It look like the sun stopped for me to get to America.

After I arrived in New York at the airport, we were separated from each other's to go on the direction they have sponsor. When he come to me they tell me I need to go to Phoenix Arizona and I was surprised because I have sponsor from Los Angeles California and from Portland Oregon I don't have sponsor from Phoenix I never heard about that city. The agent I talk with had an envelope in his hand, and I ask him if he had more information for me. He told me to wait and said that he will give me more information later. He came back opened the seal of the envelope for me and give me the name and the address of where I needed to go. It seems that he was my sponsor. I quickly wrote the information on a paper in case I needed and put the paper in my packet. I was happy to find that I didn't need to go to Phoenix by myself, and I found another young man who is going to visit his brother who live there.

Because they didn't have a plane to fly to Phoenix that night, they took us to the hotel. They said that will bring us to the airport in the morning before our flight to Phoenix. It was good for us to see the city of New York at night time. In the morning they took us to the airport to the terminal when we take the fly for Phoenix. After I entered in the plane I change places with somebody to set by my friend which I meet in New York who is going to Phoenix with me. We had a lot of fun talking on the plane. He noticed that I was little worried because I don't know anybody in Phoenix, so he tried to comfort me a bit. He told me that he has a brother who is Christian too. He said that he is waiting for him at the airport.

My new friend also assured me that his brother would help me with anything that I may need to help me get started off. The time passed very quickly with us talking the entire flight. When we got off the plane we looked around to see if I saw anyone I might have known or at seen some body with the placard with my name on it but I don't see. My new traveling frind told me to then wait right here in a seat. He said that he was going to go and find his brother and then return for me after he had found him. After he left I never saw him again. Maybe when he finally meet up with his brother he had gotten so excited to see him that he simply forgot all about me. I wait there for few hours and nobody came for me, and the airport start to empty out.

Before I knew it a Spanish taxi driver saw me, he must thought I was lost and because he asked me if I need any help, he ask me in English and in Spanish were I want to go. I tried to explain him how little English that I knew, but then I remembered the information that I had written in New York. Praise God! I took the paper out of my pocket and I showed it to him. He realized that I wanted to pick up my luggage. So he took me to a place where I could get my things. He picked up few more people together and we followed him to his car. When we got out from the building it was like I was walking into a oven. It was sometime in July and it was nearly over a 100 degrees. After we found his jeep we opened the doors to let the car air out and then we were off. First he took every body home. He saved me for last, probably because I was the farthest to take home. I was exhausted, after we reached the address that was on my paper he stop the car. I hopped down from the car and went to knock on the door, but nobody came to open it. I knocked on the door several times, but no one showed. So the driver called me back to the car. When I saw no one is coming I just thought that maybe I got to get back to the airport and try to call another sponsor, maybe one of the ones that I had from Los Angeles or Portland. Maybe they could help me. I stopped knocking, turned around and with tears in my eyes I asked God for help. When

I raised my eyes I saw a lady over the fence on the neighbor's house who was dressed up like a Romanian Christian lady with scarf covering her head and I realized that she is Romanian. Without asking the driver I went by the fence and I salute her in Romanian language "Pacea Domnului" (The Lord Peace) and she say "Pacea Domnului" - praise God! I told her that I was looking for Pastor Tudor. She said very happily that he is my son and he live right here, then I excuse myself I go back to the car where I then payed the driver. I took my things and thanked him for all of his help. I returned to the lady's house where Pastor Tudor lived. I don't know I misspelled or the organization had the wrong address and apparently I was knocking on the wrong door. I had been knocking on the neighbor house but the Lord helped me out. He performed a miracle and brought the sister out in the middle of the day with all the heat at the right time. Praise be to God! I went to her house and she called her son who came home from work. We are happy to meet each other and he apologized to me for the confusion because the organization call him few days ago and told him about me which he need to pick up me from the airport on noon time, and in the morning they call him again and tell him he need to go the airport on evening. He was thinking the organization talked about one person named Constantin and was thinking the flight time was change, but actually there was two of us, it was just our last names were different. He felt very sorry for not to come after me to the airport but I was glad God make a miracle for me to find them. We exchanged few thoughts and had to go to the airport and pick up the other Brother, Constantin, who came tonight. I actually had meet the man from the camp of Latina. We went to the airport were we met with the other brothers and sister from the church who have come to expect Constantin, they have very nice habit when they expect some body to come in America they go to the airport with the all church. After we pick him up we go to this wonderful family who hosted us for several weeks and me and Costel [his short name] became good friends.

Many have compared America with the land of Canaan because it's a blessing and has wonderful people always smiling ready to receive some immigrants from any country in the world regardless of race, color or religion which we don't have something like this on earth. I said America is like the city of refuge that was ordained by God for those who are persecuted in the world and here God give them protection, and a new chance to start a new life. I have compared the ocean crossing with crossing the Jordan River where Israel made a vow to serve God. As many have made a vow that if God will help him escape and get here then they will do the will of God and they shall serve the Lord all their life. I take this opportunity to ask you if you kept your vow which you made when pass the border or when you pass the ocean when you ask him to help you when you promise him you will serve him all your life, he has heard and helped you, and now you can confess everything he did for you and you need to renew your vows as your commitment to serve the Lord. He is always by us to help and support us when we go through trials he is ready to answer our prayer, don't forget that my beloved.

The Biggest Decision

As for crossing the Jordan. "After the death of Moses the servant of the Lord, it come to pass that the Lord spoke to Joshua the son of Nun, Moses assistant saying; Moses My servant is dead. Now therefore, arise, go over the Jordan, you and all the people, to the land which I am giving to them-the children of Israel."

Joshua 1:1-2.

They were now on the hardest point on the biggest decision of their lives, it is one think to dream about it and is quite another to make it really work. Each of us reach a point in life where we have two options to move forward by faith to benefit from the promises of God that is to pass Jordan River by faith like Israel did, or to accept to lose to kip what you have and stay there because it is hard to go into the unknown without faith. Jordan can be a lots of things, can be a time of incurable suffering, financial impossibilities, and family problem or even to immigrate to a foreign country like us to go in unknown where you have not been before. In all of this is a line of separation that divide us from the promise, it is a Jordan some time in our life when we have a great decision to make and we need to act by faith, you believe in yourself or if you believe in God, and if you believe Him you need to act by faith and put yourself and your situation in God hand. How long to pass the Jordan?

First of all we need holiness." And Joshua said to the people; Sanctify yourselves, for tomorrow the Lord will do wonders among you." Joshua 3:5. In other words we need to repent about anything what we did in our life we need to be clean no wall between us and God.

Next we need to have a good vision. One cannot switch his vision for another vision that's not enof. If we look in the Scripture we see the men of God which they overcome by a vision of Godly faith. Another thing we need to have is to have a total dependence on God by faith. The ark of the covenant was brought to Israel in Jordan river, which represent the presence of God and His power His glory to strengthen Israel's heart to trust in God and in His power and not in ourselves. Then we find that the priests were barefooted which I believe represents a self-denial and faith in God. We find places in the Scripture when God said: Take your sandals off your feet, for the place where you stand is a holy ground. The presence of God make even the ground holy.

Only on the priests that bare the Ark of the Covenant rich the Jordan River and when their feet dipped in the water's edge. The waters that come down from upstream shall be cut off to let the people cross over. The priests must have enough faith to reach the waters with your feet and then God does the rest. The problem with us is that we want Victory before going to the fight we want to see the end before you start. God only gives us what we need and have to work through faith. Another thing you learn here is that Israel had to keep a space of two thoU.S.nd cubits away from the ark away of Him and He will show you the way you're supposed to go because you have not passed this way before. God know everything, He know the time, and when you receive a signal by faith you need to act and the Lord God will bless you and you will see the salvation from any problem you may have. Lord give us strength to trust in You.

Amen!

"Be faithful until death and I will give you the crown of life."

Rev 3:10

Chapter 8

A New Beginning

"And He said; Do not lay your hand on the lad, or do anything to him; for now I know that you fear God, since you have not withheld your son, your only son, from me. Then Abraham lifted his eyes and looked, and there behind him was a ram caught in a thicket by its horns. So Abraham went and took the ram, and offered it up for a burnt offering instead of his son. And Abraham called the name of the place, The Lord Will Provide, as is said to this day, In the Mount of the Lord it shall be provided."

Gen 22:12-14.

After arriving in Phoenix I was in need of a few things to start my life here in the U.S. and of course the Lord take care of that. The Lord touched the Tudor family to help me and take me to their house where I lived like a part of the family for more than two weeks. He asked me what my profession was and what I want to do here in States. They asked me many questions in order for them to help me a little bit better. They also tried to explain the disadvantages that I would have while applying for work in town because neither Costel nor I knew how to drive more or less own a car. We also didn't speak English. Because of all these things the family predicted that any job we would apply for would pay us very little, and on the top of all of this he need to take us to any job we received and bring us home every day.

The Pastor said that he would do this until we have enough money to buy a car and learn how to drive and received our diver license. He told us that he had an upholstery business and if we would like to learn how to upholster furniture temporary until we learned English and found a better job. I was so happy to hear that and I considered it a blessing to be able to work for him and I agreed. When he asked me about the salary I told him I didn't have any claim. I reassured him that I was grateful for the opportunity to work, and learn from the him. I told him that all that he has done is good enough for me, but if he wanted to pay only if I make him a profit.

After two weeks we moved into a house like duplex with two apartments. The home was located in the same building that the upholstery business was located, and again it was a blessing to live there and work there. At the same time God helped me up to spiritually prepare to study the word to learn poems that I love and to recite them in a church. I learned how to upholstery very quickly and the family played me more than I could have ever expected. I was able to save some money until my family came from Romania. I worked every day and on evening we would gather together to pray, and go to church on Sunday with Brother Tudor and his family. In the same house on the second apartment lived a young christen family from Romania Petrisor, and his wife. They helped me after I moved there to go shopping and go to church because I didn't have car. After almost a month I spoke with him and I told him that I wanted to by a car to be able to go to church, and shop alone. I was not wanting to always count on others help me all the time. He promised me that he will go as soon as he had more time.

In the court yard where I lived had an underground, tornedo shelter built from concrete. There was one bedroom and a restroom where another Romanian lived, his name was George. Because we live in the same yard we meet from time to time and he was very nice to show me few places around. God had also put it in his heart to teach me how to drive. I had never driven in my life. One evening when everyone came home he called me out, and because we have a big parking lot he told me he want to teach me how to drive. He said this is one of the most important things I needed to know in America. There were only a few things he had mentioned he said the most important things were to know how to drive a car, to own a car, and most importantly to have a job. When I got out we walked to his car and he show me everything I need to know about the car. We went inside the car and he showed me all the instruments. He taught me how to turn the engine on, how to drive, how to use the signal lights left and right, he showed me how to adjust the mirrors, and he showed me how to park and how to turn off the engine. We were out learning the knowledge of a car within maybe thirty minutes.

The next evening he came back again but this time he put me in the driver's seat and tested me to see if I learned anything. He told me to start the car and to drive slowly forward and in reverse. He told me to use the signal lights on left, and the right, he also sent me driving around in a circle. Then finally he told me to park the car. We did this for about another thirty minutes. After few days Brother Petrisor came over and asked me if I'm ready. I asked him ready for what? He said that he wanted to take me to go with him to see some cars like he promised once before. I took my money $900 which I saved from my job in Italy, and went to a dealer that he knew. There was a lots of cars but I only found one that was slightly in my budget. It was an Old mobile Cutlas Supreme which was the cheapest car that the dealer owned. They asked for $1500 and Brother Petrisor then talked to the owner to try and negotiate with him. He told the dealer that I had just arrived in the U.S., and all I had was $900. He told the man that I needed the car for work. The dealer then decided to give me the car including everything that comes with it. Praise God that Brother Petrisor came with me.

When I went to the dealer I don't thinking too much of what I need to do because I was not sure if I would even find a car with the little money I have. Now that I bought the car and my brother said that I needed to take home. He told me he that he will go ahead and I will follow him. There was only one problem, didn't have a driver license, and I had never driven on the street in my life. The only time I practiced was that hour I was taught with my neighbor Mr. George. Broather Petrisor insisted that it is very simple, he said the car is automatic and easy to drive. He assured me that all I needed to do was drive slowly and follow him. He convinced me with his insistence, so I went in my car and started it up. He drove ahead of me first and crossed across the street on left hand side. When I was ready to go with my car it stopped, I started it again and prepared to cross the street on left but I don't see my brother I drove slowly on right and not too far he wanted for me. So I went slowly after him and with God's help I got home.

It was not too far from my house but when I drove my car home for the first time on street I was so nervous and sweating.

Every day I decided I would go out and practice driving, I would drive to the store, and to the church with Brother Petrisor.

I did it this way because I wanted to be more independent and didn't want to depend on someone for long time even the brothers were full of love and was always ready to help me out. After I learned how to drive I asked Brother Tudor wife to come and translate for me to take the test. With her help translating I got my driver license praise God! The city of Phoenix was a time of preparation first for material things and the Lord put in the mine of this family love to help me out and give me opportunity to learn the upholstery business job. All of this helped me out later on to take care of my family. It helped me open up an upholstery business where I worked for more than fifteen years praise God! Phoenix was a time of spiritual preparation and felt that the Lord has a plan for me but still did not know how and I pray for this. One day I meet with Brother John who was also looking like me and we met often in prayer and study the God's Word together. In Phoenix I met a beloved Brother Peter. He expected his family to come from Romania like me, and we met on the weekend and some time we drove two or three hours to a creek in California where we eat together. Sometimes we would even put our feet in the water and have a good time because was there wasn't any rivers in Phoenix and we loved it very much.

One time the church decided to make a trip to Grand Canyon. I was told that the Grand Canyon was one of the greatest wonders of the world because it has been proved to be the place of the lowest depths of the earth. We took some food so that we could eat at the top of the Canyon. When we got there I was amazed by such a true beauty. We spent the entire day there at the Canyon. We went looking around and when the church started to prepare the food, I my Brother Costel, and Brother John all decide to descend down to the river. The river which was maybe five to ten miles down the canyon, and up to half of the road was winding. And so we got halfway, fairly easy to travel down, however when other tourists were passing us on their way up the Canyon they would ask us, "Are your feet not in pain? Do you not care for yourself well enough not to go down this Canyon?" The Canyon was so difficult to travel down through that however until many people only made a few miles down before they decided to return to the top of the Canyon. People admitted that it was almost impossible go down the Canyon and then return to the top in the same day because many would start to feel fatigue. People had rumored that those who travel all the way down to the river would usually prepare a camp to stay a few nights until they regained their strength and energy before climbing back up.

I had managed to get down the Canyon within probably eight hours. The River was beautiful, we drank from the water, as it brushed against the rocks ghastfully. The water was so cold, and refreshing. We washed our faces by splashing water to our skin, as we looked up from the river we noticed how far down we had traveled. After a few moments of resting we began feeling hungry, and existed. We didn't have any strength. Falling on our knees we decided to pray. We prayed to God asking him to give us strength, to help us just as he helped the prophet Elijah. When Elijah was in trouble and hungry, God feed him on the brook of Cherith in 1 Kings 17:1-6. After we prayed I turned around to admire the river once more. As I stood by the river my eye caught the attention of a gold rock. So I ran to see what it might have been. I took one piece of the rock and on the bottom of the rock reviled our miracle. I had found three cans of pork and bean. I took the cans to the boys, with a sharp stone that I used to break the top of the cans. We asked for the Lords blessing and thanked God for the meal he had provided us. The canned food was so tasteful and filling. We thanked God once again for him giving us the nourishment to give us strength. It was a miracle at the bottom of the earth between the rocks.

We stayed there for less than half of hour, before we left I returned the gold stone exactly where I found it before so that somebody else could also receive the Lords blessing. I believed God answered our prayer and He made this miracle to trust in Him in any circumstances to see He take care of us and also to eat and get strength to be able to climb back. After we ate we received energy in our body and gained a greater faith in our soul seeing how God performed a miracle gave us food in the bottom of the earth. After our meal we climbed up half of the way right before it got dark. Unfortunately one of my friends were not able to travel as far as we did, he felt weak and exhausted. So we returned to him and helped him walk up with us. We knew that the temperature was dropping throughout the night so we decided that if we stayed togather we could keep one another warm and survive. We hear people crying and asking for help in the middle of the night because they were not able to climb up any more especially the women. They had only climbed half of the way and didn't have strength to keep going any further.

The Canyon did have an emergency rescue man. He came almost half way down the winding roads to assist people get to the top. However he can take only one person up at a time because he only had one donkey to carry, and soon we dont hear from anybody, because everybody was out from the canyon. We were the last remaining and because it was late at night it became very cold in some places. We even found ice where the sun couldn't reach throughout the day. We start to climb further and further. At times we took pieces of ice to help hydrate ourselves throughout our tedious journey. I was afraid if we sat down we are not going to be able to walk again because of our muscles. We knew if we stopped that the muscles will begin to stiffen, the worse part about our muscles stiffening would be that we could no longer walk due to the pain. If we couldn't walk, we could possibly starve to death. Looking up at the moon light it seemed that we are almost there but because of the path which was going in zigzag, we knew our journey could take hours.

Finally after the midnight we reach the top we was out of the canyon after twelve or fifteen hours praise God! When we got there on the top there was a restaurant where my car was parked. By the time we reached the top we were exhausted with hardly any energy. We didn't even have the energy and go to the restaurant. With great difficulty we reached the restaurant, we order hot coffee. After our time to regain some strength we went to the car to return to Phoenix. This trip turned to be for me a great experience with God. I learned that that when one gets to the bottom in humility without any resources and power you turn to God. You turn to God where you can put complete trust in Him. When you pray and ask Him for help He is ready to make a miracle for you. He is ready at any moment to help you out. Our problem is we are not going to the bottom in humility and we are not trusting God completely that is the reason we don't see many miracles happen in our everyday lives. God lets us to take care of ourselves but all who go down to the bottom in humility God will bless them all the way up back to the top of their Canyon of any issue.

Phoenix was a great city for me. It was the first city in America where I lived for an entire year. It is the place where I met my dear brothers filled with the love of God. I will never forget them, God bless them all! This is funny, when I was there in Phoenix many times I was thinking because the city was surrounded by barren deserts and what will happen if the power was cut off for some reason, then we wouldn't have any food, water, air conditioning, or even gas for our car, we could have died there. We would not be able to do anything. But at the same time I was thinking what the word of the Lord says:

> "Do not remember the former things, not consider the things of old. Behold, I will do a new things, now it shall spring forth; shall you not know it? I will even make a road in the wilderness and river in the desert."
>
> Is 43:18-19.

And this was rely happened with Phoenix as a desert and was flourished in recent years and the city was raised overnight and indeed was a way in the wilderness a rivers in the desert.

Now directed by the Holy Spirit I want to say something about it. For me Phoenix meant a new beginning with God through faith. We find many examples of people in the Scripture who overcome with God by faith: Shadrach, Meshach and Abednego in the fiery furnace, Daniel în the lion's den, David with Goliath, Gideon and Madianiti. Maybe you had a question on your heart if God can save you, and I tell you, yes He can and He will. Let us go together to the man of God Abraham which was tested by God and he learned that God care for him.

The Lord Will Provide

In Genesis 22 we find the story of Abraham in which God asked him to sacrifice his son Isaac on the Mount of Moriah:

"Then He said, Take now your son, your only son Isaac, whom you love, go to the land of Moriah and offer him there as a burnt offering on one of the mountain of which shall tell you."

Genesis 22:2.

God test Abraham and wanted to teach him a lesson to trust God who take care of him. This is a wonderful story and we can learn a lot from it but I jest stop on only three things that is fit to my story. God has provided exactly what was needed.

When Abraham was about to slay his son Isaac, God stopped him because He saw his faith and said: "And He said, Do not lay your hand on the lad, or do anything to him, for now I know that you fear God since you have not withheld your son, your only son, from me. "

Genesis 22:12.

Abraham looked up and saw a ram and so Abraham took the ram and offered it up to God instead his son. Abraham name that place "The Lord will provide." God has provided exactly what Abraham needed a ram to be the burnt offering. God has prepared the exact spot.

God not only prepare the burnt offering the ram, but He prepare the exact spot where he need to bring the offering on God Mountain. Some time we lose the blessing the offering which we suppose to receive from God because we are not in the right place and the right time, and should to pass time until we understand to accept Him by faith. He is not force anyone not bless anyone by force but we must trust in Him. The Word said: "But seek first the kingdom of God and His righteousness and all these things shall be added to you."

Matt 6:33.

We need to put God first in our life we have to go to the right place and to learn to depend on God. God had a right time.

God prepare the offering, He prepare it on the right place but He was doing that in His right time. If God has delayed a few seconds it was too late and Abraham would kill his son but God come in the right time and stop Abraham and save his son. He is not too busy not be able to hear your prayer, or He is not able to help you, He is always on time. The good news is not that we have a good plan for our lives and God will bless our plan, but God has a plan for us for our family He know what we needed, where we needed and also when we needed He is allows in time. Our memory is too short and we easy forget what He did for us.

"And my God shall supply all your need according to His riches in glory by Christ Jesus."

Phil 4:19.

God have a time for every things which is coming in our live He had a time for me to be in Phoenix which was a time of preparation material and spiritual for my future life and I had the experience that God take care of me. He take care of you believe in Him trust Him and He will do the rest. Many come to America and expect God to do everything for them but the Word says:

"For even when we were with you, we commanded you this; If anyone will not work, neither shall be eat."

2 Thes 3:10.

Trust in the Lord and He will take care of you.

Amen!

"To him who overcomes I will give some of the hidden manna to eat. And I will give him a white stone, and on the stone a new name written which no one knows except him who receives it."

Rev 2:17

Chapter 9

The Spiritual Battle

"After this I will return, and will rebuild the
tabernacle of David, which has fallen down; I will rebuild
its ruins, And I will set it up; So that the rest of mankind
may seek the Lord, even all the Gentiles who are called
by My name, Says the Lord who does all these things.
Know to God from eternity are all His works. Therefore
I judge that we should not trouble those from among
the Gentiles who are turning to God but that we write
to them to abstain from things polluted by idols, from
sexual immorality, from things strangled and from
blood."

Acts 15:16-20

On American Church which we visit from time to time when I
was in Phoenix Arizona I met one sweet Christian family who
have two of daughters to Christ For The Nations Institute in
Dallas, Texas. After we talk with them when the saw us that we
have the thought for God's work we were advised that it would
be better for us to go to this school which is very good for those
who are called into the ministry. I thought that the Holy Spirit

teaches us and not need people to teach us the Word of God but because I like to work for God in ministry and because they insist I tell them I will ask the Lord about it. I talk with my Brother John and I say I will not ask the Lord right hire in Phoenix because they all reedy know but I think is biter to go to California where they don't know anything to ask the Lord if is His will to go to this school or not.

He agree with me and we decided to go Los Angeles, California where his sister lives there with her family. I took off from work and we went by car to Los Angeles a journey for about six hours through the desert. They receive us very well they hosted us a few days but we don't tell them the reason before we want to have a Word from the Lord, every night we go where the Christian have mitting's for prayers but I don't have no answer. In the last day when we was ready to come back home to Phoenix the phone ring and some body call to let the family know they have prayer miting in their place, because some prophets come there from another city. This family insisted for us to stay one more night and we can go in the morning and I look to Brother John and we booth agree.

When I entered the house, they were already on their knees in prayer and we go down to and start to pray and in that moment when I put my knees down a brother prophet laid hands on me and said; You that you asked me and say in your heart that only if I talk with you will understand and accept. Yes say the Lord go to that place where they call you because that is my will for you to prepare you for my work and you will see things that you have not seen and you will hear things that you have not heard them. And other words of encouragement to strengthening my faith exactly what I ask for. I was amazed by the work of the Holy Spirit was exactly what I ask for and I understood that is God will to go to Christ For The Nations in Dallas. We praise God for His goodness we stay overnight with this nice family and left in the morning to get back home.

After I told my brothers in Phoenix, some was sorry because they wanted me to stay in Phoenix and tries to convince me that the Lord send me there and I need to work there, but after I tell them about the word I receive from the Lord they accept it and also tell me if you go to Dallas you can open a church there, which was like a prophecy because later one was come to pass. We both had cars and first we make the cars ready get the tune-up, take our staff we salute our brother we pray ask God for protection and drive one behind another on the road to Dallas, Texas a trip of maybe a thoU.S.nd ml. When we are tired we pull over to the rest area get some rest and go back on the road again. Generally the road was ok but maybe on a half way to Dallas the bearing of my tire wheel got broke and we need to wait few hours until we find an auto shop to fix it, and be able to go on the road again. With God help I got to CFNII and the students was in vacation but still they are able to give us a room on the boys building until my family will come from Romania because I expect them to come maybe in a month or so.

When I started the school I was amazed by all the organization of the school about the students who are prepared for the work of God to go all over the earth, about mom Lindsay she was a special faithful woman of God like a mother for students who after her husband Gordon Lindsay die she remain in his place and was an good example for her children's, devoted for the God vision and for the all school. The school had a very good teachers dressed with great wisdom and knowledge about the Word of God, I was never tire to hear them. On the top of it I cannot forget Brother Denis Lindsay which from the beginning I like him very much even he was the son of Gordon Lindsay who founded the institute he was a humble man of God and he was an example for teachers and for students and late one he became the President of this institute one of the best Christian institute in the world because from this institute for more than thirty years is going out hundreds of teachers preachers and missionary all over the world.

Everything was so nice but one thing I do not understand and I cannot agree with it and I was ready to quit the school, but I think is biter to wait for my wife and my daughter to come and we go together. Coming from another culture from a traditional church I cannot understand the clapping of the hands, the dancing, to shot or to whistle in the church, on our culture only the people from the world clapping hands or dancing but not in the church. I grow up in a spiritual church in a good church where the humility was like a foundation on the top of it we need to build by faith: man without tie, no long hair, no hand clock, sisters need to have head scarf, no makeup, no jewelry, no gold rings or chains, no high heels, no expensive clothes no man clothes and I cannot understand how can all of this can be unites with our faith in God. I have the spirit of judgement I judge my brothers in my heart, when I saw them in the parking lot playing when they hear the music they start to dance and speaking in tongues and I considered this taking the name of God in vain.

Before my family come I receive two bedroom apartment on King's House on CFNI campus, and when the time come I got to the airport and we met again with my wife and my daughter after almost two years and bring them home very happy praise God. I was waiting for my wife to come and see what she think about the school, and make the final decision what we need to do. But for my amazement my wife and my daughter love the school very much and want me to stay to the school, but I continue to judge them and was very hard for me for the first three months. After three months in one Sunday on worship time was a special presence of the Holy Spirit like never before almost all the church was on fire with the hands up to God with tear on their eyes, some dens in the spirit some stay on the floor, and I fill the presence of God He open my eyes and I saw the angels of God dressing in white robe on the top of the church holding hands and dance before the Lord and without knowing I start to dance before the Lord and I was fill with the love of God. From that time the Lord take the judging spirit and I was looking to the church the teachers the students with other eyes now I was sorry was because not able to do like them and I love them all very much.

Christ for the Nations was one of the most special place from my life and I cannot forget. The same way was my wife and she was very happy because she influence me to stay and I'm thankful to her to. Christ for the Nations is the college I recommend to my daughter she is the second generation graduate from it, and I recommend to all the youth who have heart for God works and need a vision or for any age to grow up in Christ and stay close to the Lord. *Christ For the Nations* open theological institute in Romania to and now the Christian from Romania are able to learn the Word of God prepare for the mission field. As I said coming from a different culture and tradition from the beginning it was very hard for me to understand and even less to receive this kind of worship, I was fighting in my spirit until God revealed to me. I believe they are a lots of Christian like me coming from different culture in U.S. and on they see the American Christians how they dress or how they worship they have problem on first. But let see few things what the Bible tell us about the truth worship.

The Secret of God's Presence

Sure there are many religions on earth and every one of them have a some cain of tradition of what they learn is and they now practice in church that is the reason we have so many religions on earth. Some of this traditions are more close to the Word of God then other. The religion was good because preserve the Word of God, without religion was impossible for the word of God to come to us today for hundreds of years. But God is sovereign and He want more from us then a cold religion with all the traditions and the rituals learn from some body, not mother how good they are in our eyes or how close they are to the Word of God. God want to have a fellowship with us, and so far no religion on earth with all the tradition on earth with all the rituals and customs they failed to bring God in the church or to keep Him there. I want you to come with me to the Scripture to see what God wants, what please Him, and how He want us to be to please Him. The Scripture says:

> "After this I will return and will rebuild the tabernacle of David, which has fallen down, I will rebuild its ruins, and I will set it up. So that the rest of mankind may seek the Lord, even all the Gentiles who are called by my name, says the Lord who does all these things."
>
> Acts 15:16-17.

I believe when the Lord say I will rebuild the Tabernacle of David He referee to the Worship. Why the Tabernacle of David was the favorite before God, and again I believe because of the way of worship. The passion or the palace, today many have the vision that the church need to be the most beautiful building in the most beautiful place to have the most beautiful chairs and windows and to have the richest and more educated person or the more nice looking to be the lider the pastor of the church. But in fact God does not come down to us for any of these reasons He is comes for our worship and He is not interesting in our building or our traditions and rituals and not even in our preachers not matter how smart they are. It is interesting how awesome the Solomon Temple was build and the Tabernacle of Moses which was built exactly after the Word of God and on the end God say I will rebuild the temple of David and not any of them what can be the secret. Where the Glory is the Tabernacle of David was favorite before God because it was based on a true worship. He learn how to persuade God to bring His presence and walk among people, find it in his wonderful psalms that he wrote to thank God.

When David talks to bring back the Ark to Jerusalem he was not so interested in gold but he was interested in the Glory of God coming down between the wings of the cherubim on the mercy seat and more than the things inside the ark. That is the reason when he bring back the ark to Jerusalem he dance before the people full with joy that the presence and the Glory of God is back again. David was a man after the heart God's, that says: "I have found David the son of Jesse, a man after My own heart, who will do my will."

Acts 13:22.

We know that the ark in the Tabernacle of Moses was places in the most holy place after the veil that separated the holy place of the tabernacle from the most holy place. In the tabernacle of David was no veil and the presence of God was with the people. After the fall of the tabernacle of David the ark was put back again after the veil in the temple of Solomon until the death of our Lord when we know the inside veil from the Temple was torn down in two from the top to the bottom, and the door was open for the people who want to come in the presence God. I believe we have the entry in the most holy place in the presence of God and I believe God is pleased to be among the people living in holiness and bring Him a truth worship.

I want God to be manifested in my heart to fill His presence. Is God presence in our heart in our family? I am sure many of us want it, but are we are ready to pay the price to let God to be manifested in our life in our church and fill His presence. Or if His presence come we know what we need to do to remain with us. David was not satisfied with short visit from the Lord he wanted much of God and some body say that David apparently has worshipers twenty four hour a day, seven days a week, three hundred sixty five days a year about thirty six years. He was an example of a true worshiper of God and he love His Presence. We limit God to a few hours maybe a seven eight hour a week. There are many churches today that have problem with the loss of their members because they lose the ability to bring the presence of God or maybe they never had it, and they continue with their traditions and rituals which they learn. Many people care about the customs of their churches more than God and His fellowship, His presence which so sweet. (So happened with the Pharisees and Sadducees in Jesus's time).

Praise God in recent years He has broken many walls of separation and many catholic churches, baptist churches and other denominations were baptized with the Holy Spirit and enjoy the Lord presence. Now we understand why God love the Tabernacle of David and why He promise He will rebuild it. We live in that time now it is up to you my dear in what are you interested, you are more interested in the religion you are born with their rituals and traditions or you are interested in the presence and the Glory of God. The Lord is interested in you not in your religion not your building He like to have a fellowship with you. The Lord enlighten you.

Amen!

"And he who overcomes, and keep My works until the end, to him I will give power over the nations."

Rev 2:26

Chapter 10

A Life of Service

"When Jesus come into the region of Caesarea Philippi, He ask his disciples, saying, who do men say that I, the Son of Man, am? So they said, some say John the Baptist, some Elijah, and other Jeremiah or one of the prophets. He said to them. But who do you say that I am? Simon Peter answered and said, You are the Christ, the Son of the living God. Jesus answered and said to him, blessed are you, Simon Bar Jonah for flesh and blood has not revealed this to you, but My Father who is in haven and I also say to you that you are Peter and on this rock I will build My church, and the gate of Hades shall not prevail against it. And I will give you the keys of the kingdom of heaven, and whatever you bind on earth will be bound in heaven, and whatever you loose on earth will be loosed in heaven."

Matt 16:13-19

Soon after my wife and my daughter come from Romania we dedicate special time to pray in Romanian like we used to pray when I was back home. We start to pray in our apartment on

King House in *Christ for the Nations* campus and then I shared this with Brother John who was also with me at *Christ for the Nations* institute. He also agreed that on every Sunday after CFNI church service we met in our apartment in King's House to have fellowship and to sing pray and share God's Word in our Romanian language in the summer of 1984. After we gathered several times I fill the desire to look for others Romanians if we find and bring them to have fellowship together. Soon we find two very nice young brothers Peter and Vasile who visited a nearly church and with God help I meet with them, I was very happy to find out that they are Christians to and we share the same thoughts to do the will of God, and of course they join us in prayer and fellowship in our apartment every Sunday after noon. It was not long and find out that in the city of Waco, Texas a sister Marioara a very faithful woman of God come from Romania with her family and she live there at about eighty mile from Dallas where we visit them and we pray, sing, confess the Word of God, and have good time together.

They tell me they find out a group of Christian gather together in Houston, Texas, and in a short time we visit them to. There I met another Brother Costel who live there with his family I know him from Latina camp in Italy. He tell me he hear that in Dallas move from California a Brother Stefan with his family which come from Romania and he give me his phone number. Again we have good time with our brothers in Houston, we invite them to come and visit us in Dallas and we return home. I was so happy to find about Brother Stefan, I met him first time on the bus in Yugoslavia on the way to the border of Italy and next in camp in Latina, I take him to work with me, and live with me and other two brother in camp in Italy. Soon I got home I called Brother Stefan and he give me the address, I get in the car with my wife and my daughter and drive to his place to meet him and his family. Was a great meeting because we met our families, have enjoyed our time together and after they find out about our meting they say they are happy to come with us.

Through them I learned that his wife had a sister Lenuta which she move from California to Dallas and later she joined us to. Not for long we find a young orthodox family Dorina with her husband and two daughter and after we met them and talk with them about our mitting's they agree to come to have a fellowship with us. In short time we find a Baptist Brother Adrian which come with Charites to Dallas and he was very happy to join us, he was a man who have the gift of singing and was a good help for us with the music. After few months in the sprigs of 1985 I receive a call from a Brother Cornel who live in Houston, Texas a brother which I met when I was there in visit. He told me that his company who he work for has a vacancy in Dallas and want to move to Dallas with his family. He ask me if I could help him to live with me until they fix the problems with the job and to find and rent an apartment to bring the family, and of course happy I tell him he will be welcome to come to my house. He live with us for about two three weeks, he got employed and then he rent an apartment close to his company and brought his wife and three children's whom he had then. In less than one year we was already four or five families and with children's over twenty five persons. Because the distance where to long for some to come every time to my house we decide to have prayer mitting's in rotation and give the opportunity to others Romanian from the area to come and have fellowship with us.

Sometime in 1985 two young brothers Zacheu and Brother Daniel come to Dallas and they come to have a fellowship with us to. After one year and half the group increase then become more difficult to gather in apartments where we most of us lived because the living room of the apartments is small and we start to pray and ask God to prepare a place for us. After we have the confirmation of the Holy Spirit through His prophets hire in Dallas we start to look around and visit the American churches and find a place to worship and found a church in a central area that would be good for all of us . Together with Brother John after we pray to the Lord we go to talk with the Pastor of Lake Wood Assemble of God on Abrams Road a great man of God that when he saw our need with love he showed us a good room on the second floor who told us you can use it on Sunday morning from 11-1 p.m. and Thursday evening from 7-9pm as was our need. The room was very good because had a outside entry from the back and not disturb their service and have over fifty seats good for us and we can use without any rent a really blessing and we praise God for it.

In February 9, 1986 we started the first Romanian church service from 11 a.m. to 13 p.m. I start the service with over twenty five persons and other fiends and with the help of the Holy Spirit the church grew very quickly as some time the Romanian friends which we bring to church was more than us the Christian. After we open, the Church decide to have a meeting with all the brothers to elect the leadership of the church and in March 16, 1986 the church elect me through vot to be the Pastor of the church, Brother John to be the secretary and Brother Cornel to be the treasurer and the name of the church will be Romanian Pentecostal church. We also decide to have the Lord Super in the first Sunday of every month in the church and to receive offering in every service and the offering from the Lord Super Sunday, the money need to give to the poor in Romania. Very soon after we open the church Brother Aurel call me from Colorado and ask me if I help them out because he want to come to Dallas with his wife and of course I was happy to help them out and they live with me for few months until I find the job for them and help them to rent an apartment close to the job and move out. Was a good family his wife sing in a church and Brother Aurel help us with preaching the word.

After them a very nice family, Brother Onescu with his wife come from California to reunite with the rest of the family which live in Dallas. I like to mention that was like the first love, we all love each other very much and barely get to meet each other in fellowship. Of course in the meantime we continued to visit the brothers from Waco, Texas who were the closest to us and we enjoy the fellowship, one time we go visit them and other time they come and visit us. Again other two faithful brothers Stefan and Mihai emigrate from Yugoslavia to Dallas and after we find them we bring them to our fellowship.

In the main time I was graduate from Christ for the Nations Institute and I was ordained as Minister by the World Bible Way Fellowship and in September 7, 1986 was serve the first time the Lord Supper in the Church praise God. Other Brother Aurel call me from Chicago and I help him few days and until he got the registration to CFNII and get a place to live and he also help us with worship in the church. And in a year or so we have Brother Mircea and his family, we have Brother Tomulet and his family, Brother Tiby, Brother George, Brother Buriman come from San Lois, Brother Stefan family from Romania, Brother Mihai family from Romania, Brother Buriman family from Romania.

In the same time The Holy Spirit move the Christian from Waco and the group start to grow up, I encouraged them to have a weekly fellowship and they call me for the Lord Supper, baptism, weddings, dedications, funerary service. Was a connection of the Holy Spirit between us, and God work through signs and wonders hire in Dallas and in Waco. One time I had to go to perform a baptism in Waco and start to pouring rain as in Texas and could not see anything in front of us, was impossible to drive the car and I could not get in time to Waco where my brothers were waiting for me for baptism. We were with my van full with brothers and sister and I told my wife which seat in the front to pray together and ask God to stop the rain, some said don't tempt God, but we go in His name and we start to pray and when we finish, the rain stop and the sun come out as like never rain and nobody can speak a word. In another time I go to Waco with my van and I have engine problem. I drive few mile and the motor stop, I started again I drive one or two mile and the engine stop again, and after is happened several times I realized that it is impossible to go to Waco this way. I receive direction by the Holy Spirit to pray and put the anointed oil in the engine, everybody come down the van, again was full with brothers and tell them what I need to do and after we pray to the Lord I put the anointing oil in the engine we go up in the van, I start the van and go eighty mile to Waco and I don't have no more problem with the car until I sold it several years later. Yes God is Great and is worthy to be praise and again God help us to go there in time and also He anointed the word and the people receive because God had a special plan with them.

With joy I serve like this for few years the church in Dallas and the church from Waco but become more hard, I was driving to Waco least one time a month to serve them at the Lord Supper and other services, and some time they come to Dallas and have service together take the Lord Supper and have a good fellowship with Romanian food. They asked me what they need to do because they need somebody to serve them between, and I tell them to pray, fast, and to ask the Lord for direction and elect one brother as Scripture say to do this job.

Sister Marioara a very faithful women of God who was also gifted with the gift of prophecy donate one of her room to use for church service. They had a meeting and elect Brother Josif to be their leader, and we appoint a day when I go back to Waco and I ordain Brother Josif to be the Deacon of the Church and be free to serve with the Lord Supper and other services praise God, and after we have good time eat together and come back to Dallas. Then even if I don't not go that often to Waco we still had good relations with Brother Josif who was a beloved brother and with the all church and we continue to work together in Dallas and in Waco for many years.

In Dallas the Lord bless me with part-time job because I was in college and after I was graduated with a full time job at the same upholstery business. When I apply for job I tell the boss that I'm a pastor of the Romanian Pentecostal Church of Dallas, and I want to work for him with one condition if he let me go from work if somebody from my church call me because he have any problem and need a special assistance. And the boss say yes, that was a real blessing because I was able to work and in the same time I was able to help my brothers. But not only that, and after work the Lord help me to visit other brothers from church or other Romanian which was come recently to America and need some help. We have church service Sunday morning and Thursday evening to the church and Wednesday night we have prayer meeting in the houses, and on the rest of the evening visiting my brothers and friends and urge the to do good and pray with them. I thank God for love, for the health, and for the opportunity He give me to work for Him, and with joy I was every time reedy to help my brother in their needs. I help some to stay in my house for few days, other for few weeks, and other few months, or years. I help them to get social security, to get driver license, to by a car, to find a job, to renting an apartment, to get passport, with emigration paper take them to school, to work, to church, this is some of them to God be the glory. And on the spiritual side the Lord work in the church and we grow more than fifteen family's around sixty persons in a short time, and the Word was empower with signs and wanders.

I remember how the Lord worked once I was on the way to visit one family in Est Dallas and the Lord tell me to turn around and go immediately to sister Lenuta in north Dallas who need help. I tell my wife and I turn the car and go faster I can to her house, and when I got there I saw that the house was on fire, I woke her up because was little late and we help her to extinguish the fire and I tell her how the Lord turn us around and send us to her to woke her up because the Lord love her and together we praise God for it. Other time I got a phone call from one Brother Mihai who live in north Dallas and he tell me he is very ill and ask me if I want to and pray for him. I call another's two brothers who are off to come with me and we gave mitting in the parking lot, and even from the parking I hear him screAmeng of pain, we go inside and we pray for him I anoint him with oil and God healed him and us full with joy start to praise God with singing and dancing and even him stand up and dancing with us.

Every time after the Lord Super I encourage brothers who have needs to come in the front and after I anoint them with oil I pray for them to get healing. I remember one time another sister Lenuta confesses how she had revelation from the Lord one evening, that if she come in the front in the Lord Day, and I anointed her with the oil and prayer for her, she will be healed. She never tell no body but wait for the Lord Supper Sunday to come and when I ask if somebody have needs to come in the front she come and when I anoint her with oil and pray for her she was move by the Holy Spirit and got heal and with all the church praising God for His Love. In another occasion a sister Mina was sick and called me to go and pray for her to get healing, she call more brother to come, and when I rich the place was more brothers around with different opinions some want to pray some don't for different reasons. If you look on her, you saw her face was change and she had pain. We sing a song read the Word of God and give few words of encouragement and faith, and I anoint her with the oil and pray for her God healed her, her face change become normal no more pain and I was able to talk with her and we praise God for this work. I serve the church in Dallas for many years in collaboration with Brother Joseph from Waco, Texasand some time with Brother Sandu from Houston, Texaswhich was more distance, for the Lord Supper, baptism, weddings, dedication of children's, funerals and other services.

After years of peace and holy joy and when we don't expect come the fire of testing. Between brothers was rise some misunderstanding, exceed some words which grow day by day and even the church start to be affected from it and was not a good example for church and in special for friends which come with us and want to become Christian. Then the church decided to take action to restore the order and the discipline in the church with peace in mind. And of course when you looking to make peace between two persons is almost impossible to not grieve one of them and that was happened to us. When the church has taken a decision to correct, some sorrow occurred but was ended well, but late some took the advantage of this opportunity I think for personal reasons and they break the church and left with half of the brothers elsewhere.

This is the saddest page in the history of the church in Dallas and I think this separation was not by the will of God, which has affected all of us up to today, because some went from one side to another, other go to American church, others have not gone anywhere for sorrow. One thing that I'm sorry about is through Dallas pass faithful brothers who had the advantage to work for peace and unity of the church most of them was looking to achieve their personal goals and they go to one group or another and they did not care the will of God and the unity of the Church. Until today is a spiritual battle that affect the entire community. I think we need to repent to forget each other and come together and ask God to forget us wherever we are, and I think the pastors and the leaders of this groups had the responsibility before God to be the first to give examples to the flock, and I'm sure the rest of the church will do the same. We don't need to do parties to favor one or the other as the Corinthians did and were admonished by Paul when he heard their conduct.

> "For when one says, I'm of Paul, and another, I'm of Apollos, are you not carnal? Who then is Paul, and who is Apollos, but ministers through whom you believed, as the Lord gave to each one? I planted, Apollos watered, but God gave the increase. So then neither he who plants is anything, nor he who water, but God who give the increase. Now he who plants and he who water are one, and each one will receive his own reward according to his own labor. For we are God's fellow workers you are God's field, you are God building."
>
> 1 Cor 3:4-9.

So we as workers need to be one and every one of us need to work with the gift we receive from the Lord through the Holy Spirit.

I take this opportunity to ask for forgiveness if I offend somebody in my years of service and if I did I just tell you before God was not my intention and also I want to thank everyone of you for give me the opportunity to serve you in one way or in another, I love you all with all my heart.

The True Church

> Jesus answered and say to him, "Blessed are you, Simon Bar-Jonah, for flesh and blood has not reveled this to you, but My Father who is in heaven. And I also say to you that you are Peter, and on this rock I will build My church, and the gate of Hades shall not prevail against it. And I will give you the keys of the kingdom of heaven, and whatever you bind on earth will be bound in heaven and whatever you lose on earth will be loosed in heaven."
>
> Matt 16:17-19.

Some have taken these verses literally and believe they found the remains of Peter and now they can build a church over them and this is the evidence that this is God church, and other went further saying, they have the keys of the kingdom of heaven and now they can bind or loose sins who they want in return for a fees of money and they make business with the church. Do you think this is was the will of God? For sure is not, and if is not then about what church Jesus is talking about when

He says: "I will build My church." To find out we go back to the Scripture:

Even from the Old Testament after the fall of man, God had a plan for humanity and if we look at the Noe's ark, the Tabernacle of Moses, the Tabernacle of David, the Temple of Solomon, the vision of the Ezekiel's Temple all speak of God's plan and direct us to the Lord Jesus and His church which will come. All of those were good in their time but have not able to change people but God on His appointed time had a wonderful plan with the Lord Jesus and His church in the last days, which the Apostles speak of it as a mystery kept hidden.

> "Now to Him who is able to establish you according to my Gospel and the preaching of Jesus Christ, according to the revelation of the mystery kept secret since the world began but now made manifest, and by the prophetic Scriptures made known to all nations, according to the commandment of the everlasting God for obedience to the faith."
>
> Rom 16:25-26.

> Or "How that by revelation He made know to me the mystery (as I have briefly written already, by which, when you read, you may understand my knowledge in the mystery of Christ) which in other ages was not made know to the sons of man, as it has now been revealed by the Spirit to His holy apostles and prophets."
>
> Ehp 3:3-5.

> Or: "The mystery which has been hidden from ages and from generations, but now has been revealed to His

saints, To them God willed to make know what are the riches of the glory of this mystery among the Gentiles which is Christ in you the hope of Glory."

Col 1:26-27.

The church of God was the hidden secret for centuries but was first discovered by Jesus when He said to Peter" on this rock I will build My church. I believe that the Lord Jesus was referring to Peter faith, in other words that the church will be built on the faith in Jesus. And as the Old Testament, Noah's ark was build according to the plan of God, as the tabernacle was build, the Solomon Temple was build and the Church of God need to be build the same way according to the plan of God which was revealed to the Apostles and prophets through the Holy Spirit. It is very important to build by the plan of God and we saw in the Old Testament when was built after the plan of God the Glory of God come down to confirm the work:

"Then the cloud covered the tabernacle of meeting, and the glory of the Lord filled the tabernacle. And Moses was not able to enter the tabernacle of meeting because the cloud rested above it, and the glory of the Lord filled the tabernacle."

Ex 40:34-35.

"Indeed it came to pass, when the trumpeters and singers were as one, to make one sound to be heard in praising and thanking the Lord, and when they lifted up their voice with the trumpets and cymbals and instruments of music, and praised the Lord saying; For He is good for His mercy endures forever, that the house, the house of the Lord was filled with a cloud so the priest could not continue ministering because of the cloud for the glory of the Lord filed the house of God."

2 Chronicles 5:13-14.

And the same way regarding to the church which is built with living stone and if is built by the pan of God we receive the confirmation of the Holy Spirit.

"In Him you also trusted, after you heard the Word of Truth, the Gospel of your salvation; inwhom also having believed, you were sealed with the Holy Spirit of promise."

Eph 1:13.

So today the Church is not a building even if we build a place to worship, but we are the church the people, and many get lost today because they don't know the Scripture and don't know the power of God or they jest receive that from the parents. We all have the responsibility to search the Scripture which is the Word of God. The church is not only one denomination is not nationalistic or Judaistica. The church are all who hear the call for repentance and they receive the Lord Jesus as their Savior whose life is changed by the Word by the Spirit not matter about the nation, color, gender, denomination, or what church is worship with. This is the church of the first born;

"But you have come to Mount Zion and the city of the living God, the heavenly Jerusalem, to an innumerable company of angels, to the general assembly and the church of the firstborn who are registered in heaven, to God the Judge of all, to the spirits of just man made perfect."

Heb 12:22-23.

The church must be; Victorious, United, Glorious;

One "You also, as a living stones, are being build up a spiritual house, a holy priesthood, to offer up spiritual sacrifices acceptable to God through Jesus Christ."

1 Peter 2:5.

"According to the grace of God which was given to me, as a wise master builder I have laid the foundation and another builds on it. But let each take heed how he builds on it. For no other foundation can anyone lay than that which is laid, which is Jesus Christ. Now if anyone builds on this foundation with gold, silver, precious stones, wood, hay, straw, each one's work will become clear; for the Day will declare it, because it will be revealed by fire and the fire will test each one's work what sort it is."

1 Cor 3:10-15.

Christ is the master builder, and the building is a spiritually one and need to build through the Holy Spirit.

"Therefore He says; When He ascended on high, He led captivity captive, and gave gifts to man."

Eph 4:8

"And He Himself gave some to be apostles, some prophets, some evangelists, and some pastors and teachers, for the equipment of the saints for the work of ministry, for the edifying of the body of Christ, till we all come to the unity of the faith and the knowledge of the Son of God, to a perfect man to the measure of the stature of the fullness of Christ."

Eph 4:11-13.

To summarise, we are the Church all who received Jesus Christ as our Lord and Savior by faith we repent of dead works, that we receive the New Testament water baptism, and receive the Holy Spirit baptism and He give us His gifts for the building of the church. If we read the Scripture and ask God for wisdom we can check ourselves first of all if we are in the faith and if the church we going to it is the true church and if help us to grow spiritually. The Word tell us the true church is built on the foundation of the apostles and the prophets and the Lord Jesus is the cornerstone. To find out more about the New Testament church it is good to start reading the Acts. It is not matter what church you going to if the church teach the water baptism the baptism of the Holy Spirit, the gift and the fruit of the Holy Spirit and they are manifested in the church to grow and help other than is true church if not then look for a good church to enjoy and help you grow. The Lord help you.

Amen!

"Behold I am coming quickly! Hold fast what you have, that no one may take your crown."

Rev 3:11

Chapter 11

The First Mission to Romania

And He said to them. "Go into all the In My name they will cast out demons; they will speak with new tongues they will take up serpents; and if they drink anything deadly, it will by no means hurt them; they will lay hands on the sick, and they will recover. So then after the Lord had spoken to them, He was received up into heaven, and sat down at the right hand of God. And they went out and preached everywhere, the Lord working with them and confirming the word through the accompanying signs."

Mk 16:15-20

Even if I work with to the church in U.S., I still had the thought of the mission and we pray for Romania and we help the Romanian brother when they were in need. I always remember when we are visited from American brothers who have sold their home and left to go on mission field in Romania I felt the most humiliated that I could not do it for my people and they can. I manage to get back to Romania only after ten years after the fall of communism, I really wanted to meet with my loved ones for long time, I was not able to communicate with them, and so much more to tell them about the love of God because I don't want them to be fire from the job because of me.

First visit I made in 1992, when I flew to Germany we rented a car and drive through Austria where we visited a Romanian church in the southern region where we enjoyed for a week with brothers from my own town which we know from Romania. After that we pass to Hungary and drive to Romania, even from the border we can figure out the big weight which was in Romania, hundreds of people standing in a row at the border with Hungary to make some business, they pass in Hungary and sold some staff and bought something else and returned back in Romania with bags over their shoulder.

When I entered in Romania the roads was very bad with large pits and the divers go around them, everybody drive how they can, need to go around people, animals and even other cars stopped in the road. From Arad I went to Deva on the Mures valley and on the evening was come down a very thick fog that I could not see two feet in front of my car. Many pulled over and waited until morning that they could go on. It was very hard to stay there overnight when I know few kilometers my mom and my sister is waiting for me which I have not seen them for more than ten years, so with great difficulty I drove all night through the fog over hundred and twenty miles and in the morning I arrived at my mother and my sister gate house. I pray to the Lord for my mom to resist and do not have any emotion attack when we see each other. With God help everything was OK and we all enjoyed when we met.

Every day we sing and pray with my mom and sometime come others friends of my mom from the street and pray together. One night one family neighbors how they repented after I left Romania they invite us to a prayer meeting in their house. With me was my brother-in-law, and without realize when they give me the Word, the Lord used me in that evening in a special way then every soul was caressed and receive cures for all sickness and all hands was up and with tear in their eyes, even my brother-in-law who was the first with me in a prayer meeting. It was like a dream I could not figure out what happened to me but people were hungry for the Lord they were sick and need healing and He was glorified praise His Holy Name. In the same time I visited churches in Hateg and Deva and other Christian family's which I know them before I left Romania. I stayed with my family a couple of weeks in which time I visited other friends, and after I have committed them in the arm of the Lord I went back through Austria where I comfort the brothers and go back to Germany and to U.S.

In 1994 we went back to Romania and this time we have prepared in advance, my wife prepare with clothes for the poor and I prepare the medication I hear that is no drugs in Romania and I bought at a full suit case of drugs, I fill my station wagon with clothes medicine and I send him to Belgium. One month later we fly to Belgium and go to the port and pick up our car and then drive through Europe and went back to Romania. Of course after I visiting my family with my wife this time we go to a village near Cernavoda, Dunareni from county of Constanta to visit my wife sister who live there with her family. After we met we stay with them for few days and I was interested to find Christians in the area and we find only one sister in the valley but her husband was not Christian. I ask my brother-in-law to go with me and met that sister.

When we went and introduce ourselves to her she was very happy to hear we are Christian, she confess that was praying for long time before God to send Christian in hear village to help her, and she considered us like massagers send from the Lord. Praise God she have a good husband and they receive us and I ask them if they can let us to have meeting in their house and they both agree. They call all the neighbors and all who wanted to come and hear the Word of God, and on the first meeting our sister mother which was blind receive sight, that was strengthened those who was present or they hear about it. That arose a revival work and many have come to us for a week and were edified. Time was short for us but I left our sister now to find a brother to make contact and to come to assist them with the work of the Lord in that village until God will up rise some body from the village to be able to do the work of the Lord and bring the people together. Sister fined a man of God from Basarab who accept and come every Sunday to preach the Gospel to them and we support him as we could.

In 1996 after two years we returned back to Romania, this time again my wife prepare packets for each one them because now she know biter what they need and what size. When we arrive in Dunareni we can't find my sister and my brother-in-law home because every one of them was to my brother-in-law's sister's house to mourn because she jest pass away and everybody was sad. I took my Bible and we go there to find them. The house was full of people, relative, neighbors and orthodox Christian and there was no one to set them advice or a teaching in that night. One person saw me that I have the Bible in my hand and ask me if I want to tell them something from it and thus opened the door for me to preach the Gospel, we stay late to preach and many was comforted.

The next day I contacted the brothers who now had the house of prayer and we enjoyed very much our fellowship, we give them our gifts and again we stay with them for more than a week and we have meting every night and on day time we visit brothers and see their needs. This time we organize a baptism on the Danube River and even my sister in law want to receive the baptism. Was late fall and the Danube river have ice on the sore but I still perform the baptism for two sisters. Brother Milica who help the village and preach the Gospel for two years come and two others pastors from Constanta, brothers from the village, and others many people from around the village come to hear the Word of God, and see the baptism for the first time in their life. After the baptism we go to my sister in law house and my wife prepare food drink for everybody some have place to stay inside on the table and some stay outside but everybody enjoy the time and was happy praise God. Brother Milica invite us to visit his home church from Basarab where we have a good time in church and his house and we return to Dunareni where we stay few more days with my brothers and come back in U.S.

In 2005 we returned back to Romania into a short visit after my mother got heaven I visit my sister and my brother-in-law I was to the cemetery to put some flowers on her grave and on my little nice who was pass away on young age. I stay with them to comfort them after the loss of my mother, I visit the church from Hateg and Pastor Damian a great man of God. One night I ask the permission from my sister to see if we can invite and met with friends, relative with whom I grew up and have a meal to talk with them because I never met them for long time. And of course she enjoyed and had agreed but said is very difficult to bring them. I call each one of them to invite them to my sister house for dinner and to meet with them because is more hard for me to go to each one individual. Almost all of them come and the Lord worked out because they ask me about my life why and how I repent and they was so impressed how God worked in my life and even a lady tell me she never hear something like this in all of her life and we all have a good time, and some of them come to church next Sunday praise God.

I made more trips to Romania but every visit turn to be a short mission trip, and where I was every time they were souls who have receive the Lord, receive healing, they were baptized, and for all I bring glory to God who work out. I saw the need even today, people are hungry for something let us bring them the One, Who can give them Peace, Joy and Salvation. We, the diaspora, are obligated to take care for those in our country. Maybe we have more resources here to help them both, financialy and spiritualy.

To Preach the Gospel

In Scripture we find in many places where the Lord send His disciples to preach the Gospel. The Lord ordained seventy others and send them in the cities where he had to go.

> "And they said to them; The harvest truly is great, but the laborers are few; therefore pray the Lord of the harvest to send out laborers into His harvest."
>
> Luke 10:2.

He don't tell us to pray for schools, orphanages, churches but He tell us to pray the Lord to send out workers, if we have workers all of the other thinks will be done. Is over seven billion and only two billion are Christians of which only one billion is Christian Protestants. So today we see the harvest is great and we need workers.

I remember when I was a kid and lived in the country side and when the harvest was ready for reap up. The people unite together and don't have peace until they reap the harvest they help each other, working day and night before the rain come to ruin everting. So it with the work of the Gospel, the harvest is ready for reap up, we need to leave everything any occupation and to deal with the work of the Gospel that all the crop to be put in barns before the judgment that will come to judge all the sons of disobedience on the earth. We have a great gift, but also a great responsibility then let us help each other do not have peace until they all will go all in the kingdom. We live in the world with lots of problems of various kinds; Economic: as are people in the world today who cannot feed their children starving and die for the lack of food. Politic: when the people kill each other because they have different politic view. Religious: it is sad that even today because somebody had different religion view to kill each other, we supposed to be biter then unreligious we need to be an example in endurance and help each other. The last commandment of the Lord Jesus was:

> "Go into all the world and preach the Gospel to every creature. He who believes and is baptized will be saved, but he who does not believe will be condemned."
>
> Mark 16:15-16.

Are over two thoU.S.nd years since Jesus spoke these words today more than anything we need to tell people about the love of God and about the salvation through the sacrifice of Jesus because only Him He can change the heart of man. Only through His love and by His help we will be able to love ourselves and our neighbor. There are many good things we can do, but the biggest think is to be involve in the work of the evangelism in mission. Jesus give us the command" Go" in Mark 16. Looking around us we see that our nation is becoming more increasingly anti-Christ. We live in the last days, the world is going from bad to worse even churches that had once preached the Word today are in favor of abortion, divorce, alcohol, drugs and same sex marriage. Our society is full of hatred, lying, burglary, violence, crime, pornography, prostitution, only the Lord can get rid of these spirits only He can change us and only He can give us the power to be able to work for Him. All the people are lost without Jesus. Jesus Christ is the only way He is the only bridge of connection between man and God. Without Him the man cannot know God have no hope for the eternal life.

> He says, "I am the way the truth and the life. No one come to the Father except through Me."
>
> John 14:6.

Some say that the Gospel is exceeded and is old. But only Jesus can give the world peace and tranquility they needs. Read the Bible and see all the prophecies all of them that we live in the last days for that we need to preach the Gospel before is too late. We Christians have the greatest gifts given by God for this world. If faith in Jesus is alive in our hearts then it must be on our lips. We can say that like Paul the apostle:

> "He has delivered us from the power of darkness and conveyed us unto the kingdom of the Son of His love, in whom we have redemption through His blood the forgiveness of sins."
>
> Col 1:13-14.

Salvation is free and whoever prays the prayer of faith and believe in Jesus can be saved.

> "For the wages of sin is death, but the gift of God is eternal life in Christ Jesus our Lord."
>
> Rom 6:23.

God give us the Good News of the Gospel that had to go to the end of the earth. The love of Jesus for us and the love of us for Him make us to confess about Him. We must love the sinners but to hate the sin. To love is a choice. When we understand that Jesus died for our sin, then was born in our life the love for Him and for the sinners. When you pray to God and say: "And forgive us our debts, as we forgive our debtors" we have new nature, the love of God.

> "He who has My commandments and keeps them, it is he who love Me. And he who love Me well be loved by My Father, and I will love him and manifest Myself to him."
>
> John 14:21.

Paul says: I am a debtor both to Greeks and to barbarians, both to wise and too unwise. So, as much as is in me, I am ready to preach the Gospel to you who are in Rome also. For I am not ashamed of the Gospel of Christ, for it is the power of God to salvation for everyone who believe, for the Jew first and also for the Greek."

> Rom 1:14-16.

The Lord Jesus began: "O Theophilus, of all that Jesus began to do and teach, until the day in which He was taken up, after He through the Holy Spirit had given commandments to the apostles whom He had chosen."

Act 1:1-2.

The apostles continued: "Then those who gladly received his word were baptized, and that day about three thoU.S.nd souls were added to them. And they continued steadfastly in the apostle's doctrine and fellowship, in the breaking of bread, and in prayers. Then fear came upon every soul, and many wonders and signs were done through the apostles."

Acts 2:41-43.

The apostles went out and had several missionary journeys preaching the Gospel and some of them we have on the page of the Holy Scripture. Now is our time, what I do what you do, how you work with the gift you receive from God through the Holy Spirit. Ask God to enlighten you in this area, the Lord need you and like in Jesus time we can say: "The harvest truly is great but the laborers are few; therefore pray the Lord of the harvest to send out laborers into His harvest."

Amen!

"To him who overcomes I will grant to sit with Me on My throne, as I also overcame and sat down with My Father on His throne."

Rev 3:21.

Chapter 12

The American Church

"Now the multitude of those who believe were of
one heart and one soul, neither did anyone say that any
of things he possessed was his own, but they had all
thinks in common. And with great power the apostles
gave witness to the resurrection of the Lord Jesus. And
great grace was upon them all. Nor was there anyone
among them who lacked; for all who were possessors of
lands or houses and sold them, and brought the proceeds
of the things that were sold, and laid them at the apostles
feet; and they distributed to each as anyone had need.
And Joses, who was also named Barnabas by the apostles
[which is translated Son of Encouragement] a Levite of
the country of Cyprus, having land, sold it, and brought
the money and laid it at the apostles feet."

Acts 4:32-37

Even if I serving the Romanian church in Dallas, because we
have only one service for years we had the opportunity to visit
the American churches in the evening. On first I went more of
curiosity that I really must to confess our Romanian sin because

we judged the American brothers after what we saw them on TV, about their look or how they dressed but in reality was different. We found great spiritual churches which that they impressed me very much and with the God's help I want to show some aspects of American church. First America have no shortage of churches wherever you live you will find a church where you can go even on walking distance if you don't have a car. Then compare with the churches in Romania hire most of the churches is built very modest outside but inside they have everything what they need. One of the things that impress me the most was the love of brothers that they receive us from the entry of the church, which we don't have in most of our Romanian churches. They were filled with peace and joy and with smiling on their faces they invite us in, and they find us an open seat. Almost everywhere the pastor take time to introduce us to the church and they receive us with clapping hands to thank us, and handed us a card if we want to fill so they can contact us in case we need anything.

I found many good churches where we enjoy to go, on one we like the worship, on other we like the preaching, on other the teaching, on other we saw the diversity of the gift of the Holy Spirit how He work in the church. Through the Grace of God we found some with whom we got closer and we enjoy our fellowship, about whom I want to say few things. Sometime in 1985 I met a family on Christ for the Nation campus when I was student and they invite us to go with them and visit their home church called Shady Grove Church in that time.

One Sunday before Christmas we go with them to visit the church and we like it very much, after the service they invite us to go and have diner together in their house and we accept it. My wife made special Romanian food cabbage rolls for the weekend and ask me if I can go home and bring some and share with our friend and I did. I excuse myself and I drive home to CFNI campus to get the food and I quickly climbed the stairs that I live upstairs and when I unlocked the door to get in when I saw the living I step back out I could not believe it, I thought I went to another apartment. I look around to be sure is my apartment and carefully open back the entry door, in the living room we have a lovely Christmas tree with all the staff on it, the wall was with lots of cards and stars of all kinds and under the tree lots of gifts for everyone. I cannot believe but I don't have too much time to think I gest go take the food and go because they was waiting for me. When I got there I tell my wife and she was very surprised.

Later we found out who did this lovely gesture and was the two girls from Phoenix from the family, which they recommended us the school to come to CFNII. Even if we never made a Christmas tree after we repent because of our Romanian tradition from our church, however we received with joy what they did for us in special for my daughter I think was her first Christmas tree, and I pray that my Lord Jesus to reward them.

We stay with this nice family and serve the meals together we enjoyed the fellowship, knowing them better and found that they was in Romania for mission years ago, we prayed together, then I thank them very much for what they did for us and we returned home. The same like me, my wife was amazed by what she found when we get home. But this family and the church that we visited we were stuck in my mind and whenever I had the occasion we visit that church. Few things impressed me very much from this church, first sincerity, faith and love of pastor Olen who was also in Romania for mission, next was the worship than every time when I go there I cry in God presence.

In the worship time I liked very much when they bring different banners with the Name of God or some biblical promises I feel God is present. They serve the Lord Super one time a month but they have in the church every Sunday who may want to take with their family or in group with other brothers in fellowship during the time of worship. Praise the Lord for give me the opportunity in the last years to visit this church to know them more. Another things I liked from this church was the love and the interest of the church for the lost soul's not only local but all over the world because they had missionary in many country.

In 2007 we took the membership course with God help and we became member of the church. The church had the house of prayer which is open every day and everybody who like to pray and have a fellowship with brothers and stay in God presence they can go there to.

Not for long and I met Brother Gary on mission conference which the church had every years on fall we eat together on the same table. This brother stop me one Sunday after church and tell me he have from the Lord to talk with me but every time after the service he lost me. And this time he wait for me until the service was over and ask me if we can go together with our family to some restaurant and eat and will talk about it. He took us to some Mexican restaurant and there he tell me about his mission with Kairos prison ministry and he invite me to participate with them. Was something new for me and I accepted with joy, he give me the application which I need fill and send to the state to get the approval to be able to go inside. This was a very good mission, I was with the group for few meetings of training and I was amazed that was Christens from many denominations, Pentecostals, Baptists, Catholics, Episcopes,

Lutherans, which could be joined together for a good cause to save the lost souls.

When was the time to go to jail I take off from work for one week and I was every day with Kairos in jail for one full week from early in the morning and to the evening. There we met 42 person which they sign for, and with whom we ate together, we pray together, we sang together, and we shared the Word for one week. I attended many beautiful works in my life but this is one that I can never forget all of those forty two people participating who came either for food or to have been written by someone on the list and had to come, but finally confessed that they're sorry and promised to serve the Lord.

The last time when was came my turn to preach I told them that I never ever preached in English and ask them to pray for me. When I was on the pulpit to preach I saw two or three of them which they go in one corner and put down on their knee and start to pray. I receive direction from the Holy Spirit to confess about myself about the vision I have how the Lord healed me and I repent receive Jesus in my heart. When I come down from the pulpit a lots of inmates come to me with tear in their eyes, they hug me and tell me they never hear something like this in their life. Even now when I write these words down on the paper I write with tears on my eyes because I remember about them may the Lord bless every one of them. Was very hard to live them in jail, and after a sort time I receive a letter from one of them that again filled my eyes with tears and every time I read it I cry when he explain how he fill when he heard the Word of God which give him hope again, praise God.

After few months I go to the front of the church and talk with pastor BenjAmen, after I change few words with him he ask me if I want to come to the house of prayer next Tuesday and I agree. When I go there after a few songs he saw me and called me in the front, he pick up a chair and invite me to seat down on it with the face to the church. He start to pray for me along with pastor Olin and they prophesy and other brother and sister standing around they took my hands my feet's and they all pray for me and prophesy God's wonderful works that he has in plan for me and I weep in the presence of God more the a hour. All of the words I receive from the Lord was write down and part of them was fulfil and I believe and the rest of them will be in a short time.

In the fall of 1998 with God help I open an Upholstery business job which I learn in Phoenix after I come to America. There I work with my wife and my daughter was not easy in a foreign country at that time did not know English very well and don't know too much to manage the business but I open it up by faith and I learn to live by faith every day to be able to pay my bills. The blessing was because I have more freedom when somebody call me with some problem and they need help, then I live everything and I go to help my brothers, and on the job I work late to be able to get the money to pay my bills and I never apply for help to the government or to the church praise God.

I had a great experience with the clients and I had the opportunity to talk with them about the salvation of their soul. Many time I help clients and do their job for free because they don't have money or give them discount how much they want to be able to pay and be satisfied and God Bless me. I work more than fifteen years on the upholstery business and I upholstered all kinds of furniture from all over the world and the Lord bless me and I was able to pay my bills and the taxes to the state. I remember lots of time we come and pray together for a job to come and be able to pay a bill and when the client came and pay was the exact the amount we needed to pay the bill and we go down in our knees and praise God because He take care of us.

One time come to our shop a lady Mona to repair a hand bag and after we talk I realized she is Christian and I confessed to her some of the signs and wonder of the Lord and she ask me if I want to pray for her because she have some problem with the bones of the hands and after I prayed for her the Lord heal hear. She confessed that healing in her home church and she come more often in our shop to pray together. Then I don't understand but I realized later that in fact God use her because later she brought us some clients, and when I went in Romania in mission she help us to get half price medicine to get there and also she take care of our house God bless her heart. But not only that and the Lord worked through her to know her home church "Mountain Creek Community Church" which in that time they gather in the tent because the building was under the construction and pastor Robert a very special man of God and his great parents. The place of the church location is one of the most beautiful place in Dallas Fort Worth metropolis on the top of the hill, from the bottom you drive through the forest on the top from where you have a wonderful view to the Joe Pool Lake behind. That was not all but if you have the change to climb there and put your feet on the grown you felt the presence of the Lord and when you open the Bible you receive a prophetic Word from the Lord and you praise God for it. There I went more often with my family or with other brothers to pray and receive a Word from the Lord, I fill like I'm more close to the Lord there and He hear our prayers. The building of the church was finish later one and we became members of the church for a period of time, pastor Robert was an extraordinary man he was not only my pastor but my friend and I like him very much more because he love the Lord the lost souls and he have a heart for mission and he was in Romania and supported missionaries in the world and even in Romania. When we need the building because in that time we don't have he offered to help us and gave us the place to use it.

Pastor Robert come to have fellowship with us in our house when we met with our Romanians Christian brother and give us a word of encouragement. When I got to a small mission in Romania was the only church that has helped us to help others God bless them. Even now they sponsors some mission in Romania where Pastor Robert was there several time. Pastor Robert was an example for all of us for the community, and both me and my wife have lot of joy when we go to visit and met with them.

Many time I thought about the persecution in Jerusalem how brought salvation to the Gentiles because the Christian was scattered throughout, so after the problem in Romanian church God worked out to get closer with the Americans brothers and to go more in American church where I believe I grow spiritually first of all and God was worked this way to receive spiritual healing that I needed. Even if in the last time we have more tie with the American church's and go to Romania in missions trips, we still looking to help my Romanian brothers especially those who for various reasons did not go to church or to those who live around and we met every week for prayer Bible study and fellowship in our house and on the week-ed we go and help the Romanian church, and I ask the Lord to help us to do His work until He come.

The Church With a Vision

After the baptism of the Holy Spirit we find in Acts 3 that Peter and John were going up to the temple at a hour of prayer. At the enter of the temple they met a lame man who was laid there at the gate of the temple which is called Beautiful to ask for alms from those who entered in the temple. When he saw Peter and John he ask for alms. Then Peter said silver and gold I don't have but what I have I give it to you "In the Name of Jesus Christ from Nazareth rise up and walk." And he took him by the hand and lift him up and immediately his feet and ankle bone received strength and start to walk. He entered in the temple with them, walking, leaping and praising God.

This miracle bring lots of crowds and Peter had to explain them what happened preaching the Gospel. He preach and tell them, not they but God made it, and by faith in the Name of Jesus has strengthened this man which you see and know, the faith in Him give this man a complete healing you see. And then again he preach repentance and how to return to God. All of those produced disorder in the ranks of the priest who came to the captain of the temple and the Sadducees and put Peter and john in custody until the next day because was late. Many believe and the number of the man was rise to five thoU.S.nd. Peter and John were brought into their midst and then get asked with what power or in what name they did this.

"Then Peter filed with the Holy Spirit said to them; Rulers of the people and elders of Israel. If we this day are judged for a good deed done to a helpless man, by what means he has been made well, let it known to you all, and to all the people of Israel that by the name of Jesus Christ of Nazareth whom you crucified whom God raised from the dead, by Him this man stands here before you hole."

Acts 4:8-10.

And told them that in none other name under heaven given among man, to get salvation. After they had a meeting they decided to threaten to command them not to speak to anyone in this name. As Peter and John answered them, saying: "Judge for yourself, whether it is right in the sight of God to listen to you more than to God, you judge" and because of the people they let them go. After they went to their own, they raised their voice to God in one accord and say:

"Now, Lord, look on their threats and grant to your servants that with all boldness they may speak Your word, by stretching out your hand to heal and that signs and wonders may be done through the name of Your holy servant Jesus. And when they had prayed, the place where they were assembled together was shaken, and they were all filled with the Holy Spirit and they spoke the word of God with boldness. Now the multitude of those who believed were of one heart and one soul, neither did anyone say that any of the things he possessed was his own, but they had all things in common."

Acts 4:29-32.

The first thing we see in these disciples was their Unity, they was on heart one soul. How much we can do today in the world if we have unity in the church. The secret of victory is unity.

The second thing is their Generosity, no one said that the things he possessed was his own, but they had all things in common, verse 32. The third thing was the Boldness to speak, and the apostles speak with boldness about the resurrection of Jesus and a great grace was upon them all.

Among the disciples was Joses called by apostles Barnabas mining the son of encouragement a Levite from Cyprus which he sold his land and bring the money and laid on the apostles feet he was a great man and was a good example for the church. He not only put his fortune at the apostle's feet but he put also his life in the service of the Gospel to teach and to comfort the brothers. Later one when the apostles found out at Antiohia receive the Word of God they send Barnaba to encourage them because he was a man full of the Holy Spirit and faith. And a great many people were added to the Lord then he bring Paul too with him and work together for one year. Barnaba was proved to be a faithful brother a great friend and a good example for us to show us how to be a true disciple.

And we have another example in the Bible, our Lord Jesus Christ if you don't have Him like a brother, like a friend, I suggest to get Him today, all the friends or brothers you have hire on earth they live you one day but Jesus never live you. He show His love when He come and die for us on the Calvary cross. I saw our American brothers are more united then our Romanian brothers, they did not fight for position like we do, they are more generous than we are, they build hundreds of church's around the globe, build Christian college's to prepare the youth for the work of God, they build orphanages, send thousands of missionaries to the field, and they preach the Word of God with boldness. Sure they have their struggles in special in the last years, like we do, but we have lots of things to learn from each other, and I think is biter to have more close relation between us to know each other and we need to pray for each other.

Amen!

> "When you pass through the water I will be with you, and through the rivers they shall not overflow you, when you walk through the fire, you shall not be burned, Nor shall the flame scorch you. For I am the Lord you God The Holy One of Israel, your Savior."
>
> Is 43:2-3.

Chapter 13

The Last Days

"For as the lightning that flashes out of one part under heaven, shines to the other part under heaven shines to the other part under heaven, so also the Son of Man will be in His day. But first He must suffer many things and be rejected by this generation. And as it was in the days of Noah so it will be also in the days of the Son of Man. They ate they drank, they married wives, they were given in marriage, until the day that Noah entered the ark, and the flood came and destroyed them all. Likewise as it was also in the days of Lot. They ate they drank, they bought, they sold, they planted, they build, but on the day that Lot went out of Sodom it rained fire and brimstone from heaven and destroyed them all. Even so will be n the day when the Son of Man is revealed."

Lk 17:24-30

I think we live in the last days, and I want to write down few words about it, which I think will be useful for all of us. There are many books written about the last days, the coming of the Lord, many prophets have prophesied the coming of the Lord several time, other given more evidence and give the year, the month or the day when the Lord will come and this has not happened. Because of this the people become more confused and many not believe any more in the coming of the Lord. But the Bible says:

> "But of that day and hour no one know, not even the angels in heaven, nor the Son, but only the Father. Take heed, watch and pray, for you do not know when the time is. "
>
> Mark 13:32-33.

Our enemy do two things; one to make people confused by the coming of the Lord and bring lots of false prediction which are wrong, and the second to make the people believe that some think need to happened before the coming of the Lord. But praise God He left us the Bible which is His Word and if we study the Scripture we find the signs of the end time and the coming of the Lord. When we repent and get back to God almost forty years ago we heard our brother talk about the coming of the Lord and about the last days I thought that will happen in other generation in a distant time. Over time we have seen and felt that the coming of the Lord is very near. Paul say more than two thousand years ago "Salvation is more nearer to us now than when we believe", the day of the Lord is near.

Today more than any time people speak openly about apocalyptic time, or wrote books, or movie made about it, the battle between good and evil. Even the science began to be increasingly involve more in talk about a possible end of the earth, looking for alternatives like to transfer people to other planets. There are open many organization to study more options and kip statistics and see how they can kip the earth longer. Some suggest to reduce the world population because is multiply very quickly and they believe that the food will be a problem in a near future. Other looking for a way to kip the vegetation on Earth longer and fight against pollution. Other seek to reduce weapons of mass destruction as it is believed that the atomic bomb a nuclear war would destroy all the life on earth. As I say NASA is looking to find other planets to be used for the transferring people out there when the earth will be destroyed through a nuclear war or a crash with another planet (Planet X).

If you want to know the truth you must go to the Scripture which is the Word of God and if you believe then you will understand the will of God and the time we are living in. From this Word we come we the humans, and all the knowledge and wisdom so l want to go together to this world today. Sure many have say God is good and He is love and it is true, and the question arises why God allowed so many disasters happen on earth.

God created Adam and Eve over six thousnd years ago and put them in the Garden of Eden. He created them to live eternally happy there but He give them a command not to eat of the tree of the knowledge of good and evil. The serpent come and tempted them to eat saying, if you eat you will be like God knowing good and evil, and after they eat they broken God command and the sin come to this earth. Many say if God is good why He allowed the man to sin, but first of all God is the owner He is sovereign He is the Creator, and who are you or who are me to ask God why He did that or that.

After the fall of Lucifer from heaven God wanted man to be tried, He give man a free will, and let him choose He don't create a robot like we do and we program it to do some things for us, here is the wisdom of God. God is holy and He cannot unite with sin. Sin make a wall of separation between man and God. God really punish sin but He love He prepare the way through repentance to get forgiveness and again opportunity to come close with God. Let's look on God work:

1) God take Adam and Eve out of the Garden of Eden because of sin. (Gen 3:23.)
2) God judged the world in the time of Noah when the sin was multiply on earth. (Gen 7:10-24.)
3) God judged the world because of sin in the time of Sodom and Gomorra. (Gen 19:24-29.)
4) God foretold by prophets both in the Old Testament as well in the New Testament, Jesus Himself said that God will judge the world in the last days because of sin.

With God help I want to mention some of them:

"Wail, for the day of the Lord is at hand! It will come as destruction from the Almighty, therefore all hands will be limp, every man's heart will melt, and they will be afraid. Pangs and sorrows will take hold of them; They will be in pain as a woman in childbirth; They will be amazed at one another; Their faces will be like flames. Behold the day of the Lord come, cruel with both wrath and fierce anger, to lay the land desolate; And He will destroy its sinners from it. For the stars of heaven and their constellation will not give their light; The sun will be darkened in its going fourth, and the moon will not cause its light to shine. It will punish the world for its evil, and the wicked for their iniquity; I will halt the arrogance of the proud, and will lay low the haughtiness of the terrible, I will make a mortal more rare than fine gold, a man more than golden wedge of Ophir. Therefore I will shake the heavens, and the earth will move out of her place, in the wrath of the Lord of hosts and in the day of His fierce anger."

Isaiah13:6-13.

"The great day of the Lord is near; it is near and hastens quickly, the noise of the day of the Lord is bitter; there the mighty men shall cry out. That day is a day of wrath, a day of trouble and distress, a day of devastation and desolation, a day of darkness and gloominess, a day of clouds and thick darkness, a day of trumpet and alarm against the fortified cities and against the high towers. I will bring distress upon men, and they shall walk like blind men, because they have sinned against the Lord; their blood shall be poured out like dust, and their flesh like refuse, neither their silver nor their gold shall be able to deliver them in the day of the Lord's wrath, but the whole land shall be devoured by the fire of His jealousy, for He will make speedy riddance of all those who dwell in the land."

Zephaniah 1:14-18.

"And as it was in the days of Noah so it will be also in the days of the Son of Man; They ate, they drank, they married wife's, they were given in marriage, until the day that Noah entered the ark, and the flood came and destroyed them all. Likewise as it was also in the days of Lot; They ate, they drank, they bought, they sold, they planted, they built; but one day that Lot went out of Sodom it rained fire and brimstone from heaven and destroyed them all. Even so will be in the day when the Son of Man is revealed."

Lk 17:26-30.

The Word tells us that if He not spare the ancient world it will not spare us ether if we live in sin. God don't hate the sinner but He want him to turn from his evil way to live. Today still have the opportunity to receive Jesus into our heart, to repent to stop doing sin and to escape the judgement of God which will come soon to judge the sons of disobedience. Are we in the last days, I think so, therefore I want to show you some of the **signs of the last days**, things that may convince you to make a good decision for your life, and you may persuade others.

1) Signs up in the sky and down on earth.
2) The multiplication of sin. (Lawlessness)
3) The condition of Israel.
4) The condition of the Church.

1. Signs Up in the Sky and Down on Earth

Always when something important happened God used signs in heaven and on earth. When the Lord Jesus was crucified the evangelist says:

"Now from the sixth hour until the night hour there was darkness over all land."

Matt 27:45.

"Then behold the vail of the temple was torn in two from top to the bottom, and the earth quaked and the rocks were split, and the graves were opened, and many bodies of the saints who had fallen asleep were raised."

Matt 27:51-52.

"The same way happened when the resurrection of Jesus: Now after the Sabbath, as the first day of the week began to dawn, Mary Magdalene and the other Mary came to see the tomb. And behold, there was a great earthquake, for an angel of the Lord descended from heaven, and came and rolled back the stone from the door and he sat on it."

Matt 28:1-2.

With God help I want to give you some of the signs in the sky and on earth before the end time:

A) Signs in the sky:

"And there will be signs in the sun, in the moon and in the stars; and on the earth distress of nations, with perplexity, the sea and the waves roaring, men's hearth failing them from fear and the expectation of those things which are coming on the earth, for the powers of heavens will be shaken. Then they will see the Son of Man coming in a cloud with power and great glory. Now when these things begin to happen look up and lift up your heads because your redemption draws near."

Lk 21:25-28.

Just as the word to say: NASA announced that there will be signs in the sun and the moon. And starting with April 15th and October 8th, 2014, where we have total Lunar Eclipse, and in April 4th and September 28th, 2015 the same, when Moon will turn red, and also in between we have total Solar Eclipse on March 20th, 2015.

This signs are not randomly, they tell us something, is said that the moon is a signs for Israel and that the sun is a signs for Gentile.

Very interesting because all of this signs happened during one of Israel holydays. These signs was very rare, and always when was happened before, somethings happened with Israel. Was happened in 1492-93, when the Jewish from Spain receive the ultimatum to accept Catholicism or to live the country, was happened in 1948 when the Israel got the independence, was happened in 1967 when they win the six days war with his neighboring countries and won Jerusalem after hundreds of years.

I don't think even today is not a coincidence God knows everything He know what will happen, some say the Armageddon will start and they will come against Israel, other say that the rapture of the church will be soon and that is the sign in the sun for Gentiles. I don't know, but one thing we know the end is near. Also we have lots of eruption in the sun, and some people say because of the hole in the layer of the ozone which protect the earth from radiation, the ultraviolet b may come down, and many doctors say is the cause of skin cancer in the last time. And like never before we have lots of meteorites which pass by earth and the science expect one very big planet (Planet X) which will hit Earth soon.

B) Signs on Earth:

a) Wars.
> "Then He said to them, Nation will rise against nation, and kingdom against kingdom."
>
> Lk 21:10.

Exactly like the Word say in the last years we have more and more wars between nations like never before in our life and thousands of people die all over Earth.

b) Earthquakes.
> "And there will be great earthquakes in various places, and fAmenes and pestilences; and there will be fearful sights and great sings from heaven.'
>
> Lk 21:11.

Today, more than ever, we have the earthquakes is greatly multiplying and increase in intensity like the one in Haiti not too long ago which was one of the stronger in the world and has done a great damage, and the those who control the seismic systems say they expect one very big in the near future.

C) FAmene and Pestilence.
> "For the nation will rise against nation, and kingdom against kingdom. And there will be fAmene, pestilence, earthquake in various places."
>
> Matt 24:7.

For sure after wars and earthquakes we have fAmene and pestilence all the time. But today we have more and more places in the world where the people die in special children's like Africa because they don't have enough food for the children. The same think with pestilence meaning contagious sickness, and with all the money we spend to build hospitals and educate doctors and nurses, with all the medicine and vaccine we have in twenty first century we still have thousands of people die and we are not able to cure them, and we find new bacteria or new virus which we don't have medicine, to be able to kill them. I believe all of those is signs of the end time and God try to prove us He is still in control.

2. The Multiplication of Sin

Yes, without thinking too much about the characteristics of the last days, but the multiplication of sin is one of them that is the reasons God will judge the earth very soon. With God help I want to show a few of them:

A) Abortion.

After the Bible abortion is considered a crime to kill a soul even if is not born yet. Today we can say that it is ok for different reasons broken God commandment. In other words say go live your life and come back to us to help you out to be free again. In most cases they are young girls who have no money or opportunity to pay for it and they will do on our expenses pay in taxes. Was not better to teach the young people to don't sin and fear of God, then to kill the baby through abortion with our expenses and not to mention the consequences for mothers, and the sin we ourselves are guilty of before God.

B) Same-sex marriage.

Like abortion, marriages between man and man or woman and woman is abomination is sin before God. It was sin in the Old Testament: "If a man lies with a male as he lie with a woman, both of them have committed an abomination. They shall surely be put to death, their blood shall be open them."

Lev 20:13.

The Apostle Paul says: "For this reason God gave them up to vile passions. For even their woman exchanged the natural use for what is against nature. Likewise also the man leaving the natural use of woman, burned in their lust for one another, men with men committing what is shameful and receiving in themselves the penalty of their error which was due."

Rom 1:26-27.

And after almost thousands of years Paul still believe, when he wrote his epistle to the Romans say the unity of same sex is an abomination that is was a shame and I think it is a shame today before the Lord and this will attract the anger of God. I think was better if the state together with the church open more institution to help this people to be released and healed. They are many who accepted the Lord and was healed and now they have families and are happy. If some of them are seek they are a minorities and is not good to promote something which is against the will of God to attract His judgement.

C) Pornography.

It the something that we talked very little about it, but is one of the largest business in America and in the world that bring large amount of money in taxis to the government. Here we see that again the dollar is more important than the damage which pornography makes. There has never been such a thing in the world especially with the internet, now when all our young people have access to it without the parents suspect it, and the school or the government do not care to help, they are trapped in lust and became addicted, which is much worse than the alcohol or tobacco. Because of this so many things happened in the world like; prostitution, kidnapping, masturbation, sex before marriage, family violence, divorce, abortion, drugs, alcohol, sodomismul, same sex marriages, inability to learn, inability to work, inability to have a family and much more. I think it is a time to ask yourselves, we are responsible how to grow our children's, how to educate our youth for tomorrow, or we grow some handicapped.

D) Movies and digital games.

In recent years they put on market thousands of movies and digital games that corrupted the minds of our children and youth. Most movies and game promotes sexuality, violence and filthy speech. The producer is not interested in the damage that it produce but in the profit he get, and the same the government to get more taxis. And the youth seeing those every day they record in their minds and what they see and hear today they will practice tomorrow, and they became more violent, and speak bad language, no wonder so many things happening n schools today.

All of this come so fast and take the parents unprepared, and they not even know what they bout to their children and when they find out was too late. Our children are trained by Hollywood, the parents are on work and the children's stand before the TV or internet, they copy everything what they see and no body care. Hollywood teach and the parents pay now, but the government pay later and we all pay because we don't put restrictions to the Hollywood to the media what they show and what they sold to our youth.

E) The fight against the Church.

I have over thirty years since I immigrated to this country in America through a discovery of God was big difference I was full of joy that I come in a Christian country. Today the government is becoming more and more socialist and lid the people in the wrong direction. They pull out the Bible from school they remove the Bible standard of living and make new standard of freedom lid by their heart and by dollar, they remove the ten commandments, and they are looking to remove all that remind us about God about our creator in public places, lately the pastors they are stop to pray in the name of Jesus in public, you cannot speak against sin no more that you risk to be arrested, is a constant struggle against the church the family and the Christian. Does not tell you that we are in the last days, and that all of this attract the wrath of God I believe so.

F) The great international order.

Another thing which we need to think about is globalization that many people say is working today. I remember the book of

Genesis tell us that before the flood people go away from God and Nimrod with Semiramiz have decided to make a turn and his top to reach the heaven. Then people spoke one language and God confounded their languages and could not finish the construction. Their pride was stopped by God and the people were scattered on the face of the earth. Today we are looking for globalization world, forming a one world government political system, one religion, and one economic system. Many believe today that is the only way to solve the world problems. There have been so many wars because of different political views, and so many people died, as a single political system would solve the problem. As for religion the same, how many battles have been and they are even today, a union of religion they think solve the problem. As for economy we see some country are rich and other are poor, some have everything they need others starve, one economic system would bring a balance that all to have strictly necessary and will resolve this problem to.

Due to lack of faith in God people look after their wisdom to solve the problems, but God don't like that. In the book of Revelation in chapter 13 we have a Word from the Lord, that in the last days the antichrist will comes and make that all men to receive a mark on their right hand or forehead and no one can buy or sell except one who has the mark or the name of the beast, or the number of his name. Hire is the wisdom. Let him who has understanding calculate the number of the beast, for it is the number of man. His number is 666.Today we already have the microchip that can store in it all the information about you and you don't need a passport, social security, driver license and other information about your health. Today is working to convince everyone that we need it, is so many children steal, and animal lost, you don't need to have cash or credit card with you any more to be stole from you or still your identity. The Apostle John write this thing two thoU.S.nd years ago about the mark, when was no electricity, phone or something else. This is not mandatory now, even that some country already use them on their children their pets and in military. But I believe when the antichrist come he will try to unify all the world to make the globalization and he will use the microchip the mark, to control all the people from his kingdom. Remember this is the mark of the beast 666 and those who receive the mark will be judge by God and cannot be saved. Do not get it to any price. This is a signs that we live in the last days and the coming of the Lord is near.

G) Terrorism.

I believe terrorism too is a sign of decadence of the end time was start long time ago, and was more fervent in Middle East and now is go all over the world. Terrorism is used by a group of people to terrorize other peoples or a nation to get attention and to accomplish their political or religious view by intimidate others and is very hard to control them. I think terrorism is not the will of God and however used this cain of method of terrorism, if is a person, a group of people or a nation, God allow them to use this method because He want to judge them of their sin of putting themselves in a place of God to judge others. From the beginning God give us a free will and He never change that praise God, and everybody have the freedom to choose his political and religious view, and we are not allow by God to force anybody to accept our view, and on the end of the road on the Judgement day everybody will be judge by God for everything we did on earth if we did good we go to heaven if we did more bad things we go to hell. The question is where you want to go is your choice. I suggest you to ask God for forgiveness for everything's what you did and start to do good from today one. God bless you.

3. The Condition of Israel

If we think about the signs of the last days one of the place we need to look is the condition of Israel the people of God. This nation was chosen by God from all the nations of the earth to be his priests and to show His glory through them. God give them the law, the Ten Commandments, the sacrifice for sin, the holydays, give them orders how to build the tabernacle because He wanted to live in their midst, but was not possible only temporal. When people obeyed God had peace and quiet and God was with them. When they go away from God, He go away and let them to be bitten by enemy and some time they are get slave and took far in other nations. Everything that Israel did or what happened with them has a great significance for us as a church in the New Testament. There was many prophecies about the people of Israel which was fulfilled before and some was fulfilled in our generation and some will be in a near future. The Lord Jesus prophesied about Jerusalem when He says:

> "Do you not see all these things? Assuredly, I say to you, not one stone shall be left here upon another, that shall not be thrown down."
>
> Matt 24:2.

This was happened seventy years after Christ when the roman general Titus conquered Jerusalem and the temple was demolished. Today we live in the days of fulfilling one of the most important prophecy about the people of Israel:

> "I will bring back the captives of My people Israel; They shall build the waste city's and inhabit them, they shall plant vineyards and drink wine from them; they shall also make gardens and eat fruit from them. I will plant them in their land, and no longer shall they be pulled up. From the land I have given them, says the Lord your God."
>
> Amos 9:14-15.

As was prophesied over two thoU.S.nd years we see the fulfillment of this prophecy in our generation. The people of Israel start to return to Palestine from all over the earth, in 1948 they became again an independent country, in 1967 in the six days war they conquered Jerusalem after hundreds of years where they move their capital and thousands of Jewish returning home. And even with the Hebrew language God make a miracle that after hundreds of years without being used is born again and now the children can learn to read and write in their language again. As Jesus told in the parable of the fig tree so happened with Israel:

> "Now learn this parable from the fig tree; When its branch has already become tender and puts forth leaves, you know that the summer is near. So you also when you see all these things, know that it is near at the door. Assuredly I say to you, this generation will by no means pass away till all these things take place. Heaven and

earth will pass away, but My words will by no means pass away."

Matt 24:32-35.

In the last years thousands of Jews receive Jesus their Messiah and was opened hundreds of Messianic churches all over the world. I believe in our generation the Lord will return. We need to ask ourselves, am I reedy, and are you ready? It is true that the condition of Israel is a important signs of the end time and the coming of the Lord. Yes indeed Israel pass through a critical time in history that some have promised to wipe them off the map but honestly I urge you to read first the story with Israel and see what happened with those who fight against them,if you forgot what happened in the last years. Look in the Bible prophecy that in the last days God will bring many nations against Israel with a reason to destroy them. Do not find yourself fighting against God because I assure you that you lose it. The Word teach us to pray for the peace of Jerusalem. God help us.

4. The Condition of the Church

As God-chosen the people of Israel among all nations to be a kingdom of priests on the whole earth so after the hardened of their heart God in the last days, God chosen the church. The apostles of Peter says:

> "But you are a chosen generation, a royal priesthood a holy nation, His own special people, that that you may proclaim the praises of Him who called you out of darkness into His marvelous light, who once were not

a people but are now the people of God, who had not obtained mercy now have obtained mercy."

1 Pet 2:9-10.

How God spoke to Israel in ancient time by making miracles and signs to increase their faith and to teach them to depend of God, the same way He chosen the church in the last days from all the nations of earth to teach them the secret of the kingdom. He give them the Holy Spirit and clothed them with power from on high so they can be witnesses for Him on all the earth. Church as Israel had periods when they do God will and He bless them, and had periods when they go away and God allowed them to pass through suffering and persecution and the to endure of them again. Over the centuries the church has its struggles from exterior through persecution, and from inside through divisions. From exterior the church was persecuted from the leadership of the nation where they live who did not believe in God and they push the church in a corner, saying that the church has no place in politics and government then the Christians stand back, and on leadership was elected more and more people without faith without God, and they govern a people according other principle bringing persecution. From interior because was rise up many denominations that was fight against each other and the church broken and weakened spiritually. But the worst thinks the church did along the years to control the church was that they change the Theocratic system of the church which supposed to be lid by God through the Holy Spirit with the democratic system which is lid by the people with popular election or lid by one man which became the ruler of the church with no election.

The Apostle Paul tells us very clearly in Ephesians:

> "And He Himself gave some to be apostles, some prophets, some evangelists, and some pastors and teachers for the equipping of the saints for the work of ministry, for the edifying of the body of Christ till we all come to the unity of the faith and of the knowledge of the Son of God, to a perfect man, to the measure of the stature of the fullness of Christ, that we should no longer be children, losses to and fro and carried about with every wind of doctrine, by the trickery of man in the cunning craftiness of deceitful plotting, but speaking the truth in love, may grow up in all things into Him who is the Head-Christ, from whom the whole body, joined and knit together by what every joint supplies according to the effective working by which every part does its share, cause growth of the body for the edifying of itself in love."
>
> Eph 4:11-16.

There have been several revivals when the church received a new upsurge, but the enemy is seeking to keep the church divided this way he know she don't have no power. We need a great awakening in the church, that God dress back his servants with power and the church take back her role in a nation which is given to her by God. In the last century was one of the biggest waves of revival in history of the church, the church has grown and turned to repentance hundreds of thoU.S.nd, was build thousands of churches in the world, was opened hundreds of Christian schools, mission organization, orphanages, home for elderly, the Bible was printed in many languages and dialects, was send more missionaries into the world. I believe this is the sign before the coming of the Lord.

Of course if we look for the signs of the end time we need to look on the church for which Jesus come. Let's look in the book of Revelation which is a prophetic book. When the apostles John was in the Island of Patmos for the Word of God, on the day of the Lord was in the Spirit and received a revelation from God .He heard a voice speaking to him and said: "I am the Alpha and the Omega the First and the Last, and, What you see, write in a book and send it to the seven churches which are in Asia; to Ephesus, to Smyrna, to Pergamos, to Thyatira, to Sardis, to Philadelphia, and to Laodicea. And the Lord which appeared himself to John in a vision tell him the mystery of the seven churches starting with Ephesus and ending with Laodicea.

Each church was discovered by the Lord in a certain state of belief. Some say the way they are in the row in the book of Revelation the same way was the condition of the church over the years and today we are identify with the last church with the church of Laodicea. Even if that is true, I believe that the local church can be identified with one of these states of faith of one of these churches.

With God's help I want to show some of the signs of the church in the last days:

a) Falling away.

> "Now the Spirit expressly says that in latter times some will depart from the faith, giving heed to deceiving spirits and the doctrines of demons."
>
> 1 Tim 4:1.

b) Hated by all nations.

> "Then they will deliver you up to tribulation and kill you, and will be hated by all nations for My name's sake."
>
> Matt 24:9.

c) The love grow cold.

> "And because lawlessness will abound, the love of many will grow cold."
>
> Matt 24:12.

d) False Christ.

> "For false Christ's and false prophets will rise and show great signs and wonders to deceive, if possible even the elect."
>
> Matt 24:24.

e) Preaching the Gospel.

> "And the Gospel of the kingdom will be preached in all the world as a witness to all the nations, and then the end will come."
>
> Matt 24:14.

f) Lukewarm condition.

> "I know your works, that you are neither cold nor hot, I could wish you were cold or hot. So then, because

you are lukewarm, and neither cold nor hot, I will vomit you out of my mouth."

Rev 3:15-16.

We saw together some of the signs of the last days according to the Scripture, what do you think my dear reader? Have you asked yourself that question? If you think it is true, how is the state of your life?

Is Jesus your Lord and Savior if not accept Him today, tomorrow you don't know what bring.

The end is near.

Amen!

"Come to Me, all you who labor and are heavy laden, and I will give you rest. Take My yoke upon you and learn from Me, for I am gentle and lowly in heart, and you will find rest for your souls."

Matt 11:28-29

Chapter 14

The Rapture of the Church

"Let not your heart be troubled; you believe in God, believe also in Me. In My Father's house are many mansions, if it were not so, I would have told you .I go to prepare a place for you. And if I go and prepare a place for you, I will come again and receive you to Myself, that where I am, there you may be also."

John 14:1-3.

We saw in the last chapter several signs of the last days as: signs in heaven and on earth, multiplying of iniquity, the states of Israel, and the states of the church which I believe them convinced you that we live in the end time and the Lord is coming soon. The biggest event which we expect to happen soon, I think is the rapture of the church. There are many books written about this event than many Christian are confused and do not know what to think, some pastors because of many opinions they abandoned this teaching to don't go in contradiction with anybody. Some believe that the rapture of the church will be before tribulation, some say in the midst of the tribulation, other at the end of the tribulation, while other do not believe in the rapture of the

167

church, and everybody is based on some biblical texts. When we speak about tribulation, the majority refer to the week of Daniel 9:27 and in Revelation 6-19, where there will be seven years of tribulation, started with seven seals, seven trumpet and seven plagues. To better understand I want to read a Word from the Gospel of Matthew and do a comparison.

> "When the Son of Man comes in His Glory, and all the holy angels with Him, then He will sit on the throne of glory. All the nations will be gathered before Him, and He will separate them one from another, as a shepherd divides his sheep from the goats."
>
> Matt 25:31-32.

If we compare these verses from John 14:1-3 and Matthew 25:31-32 we see a big difference between them, which shows that there are two separate events.

In John 14:1-3, Jesus looking to comfort the disciple to remain strong in faith, to wait patiently after He go to the Father, and after He prepare the place He will return to receive them to be together again. Jesus says He Himself will come, He will not send His angels but He Himself will come for His Church.

In Matthew 25:31-32, we find instead that the Lord will come with all the angels for judgement and all the nations will be gathered before him, and will break up like a shepherd separates the sheep from the gouts. I think we all see hire a big difference because they are actually two separate events. It is true that in the Gospel we don't find many verses about the rapture of the church that because Jesus speak primarily to the Jews and is very easy to confuse the two, Israel and the Church. This promise is confirmed by the apostles Paul in all his letters. He say to the Thessalonians about the rapture of the church:

> "For this we say to you by the word of the Lord that we who are alive and remain until the coming of the Lord will by no means precede those who are asleep. For the Lord Himself will descent from heaven with a shout, with the voice of an archangel, and with the trumpet of God. And the dead in Christ will rise first. Then we who are alive and remain shall be caught up together with them in the clouds to meet the Lord in the air. And thus we shall always be with the Lord. Therefore comfort one another with those words."
>
> 1 Th 4:15-18.

The Word tells us that the dead will rise first and then we who are alive in Christ we who remain shall be caught up together in the clouds and so we will be always with the Lord. It is very interesting how Paul writes, he believed that during his life the Lord come, just as we expect it to. On the rapture only the true Christian will see 1 John 3:1-3, but after the tribulation after seven years when He will come again with his church, any eyes will see Him. And also in Corinthians 15 the Apostle Paul explains with what body will resurrect the dead:

> "Behold, I tell you a mystery, we shall not all asleep, but we shall all be changed, in a moment, in the twinkling of an eye, at the last trumpet. For the trumpet will sound, and the dead will be raised incorruptible, and we shall be changed. For this corruptible must put on the incorruption, and this mortal must put on importability.

So when this corruptible has put on incorruption, and this mortal has put on incorruption, and this mortal has put on immortality, then shall be brought to pass the saying that is written; Death is swallowed up in victory."

1 Cor 15:51-54.

The question is when will be the Rapture of the Church?

I heard many people say that the rapture will be in the feast of the trumpets of Israel which is every year on the fall and it is possible. We don't know when the rapture will be, but I believe will be before tribulation and will be soon. Many have made the mistake, looking on the time to predict that the rapture will be then or then and they are shame that did not happen, but the Word says:

"But of that day and hour no one knows, not even the angels of heaven, but My Father only."

Matt 24:36.

Another question why before the Tribulation?

Many believe, even here in America newest that the church must go through the tribulation to be cleaned out in this way. Yes it is true that the church was persecuted even today in many country the church is persecuted but I'm not talking about that I'm talking about the great tribulation of seven years of trouble as I said before. I want to show you two reasons:

The first reason: If we look in the Scripture we see how God works when is come to judgement. When God decided to judge the world because of sin during Noah time, God prepares the way of escape first. He commanded to Noah to build an ark and only after the ark was ready and Noah and his family was in the ark only after that the flood came and destroyed them all. When God decide to judge the Sodoma and Gomora because of their sin God send His angels out there to take Lot and his family out, and only after that fire and brimstone came upon them and killed them all.

So I believe as God did in the old days will work on the end time when the great tribulation come to judge the world. I believe first the church will be caught up and only after the church is in the place which Jesus prepare for her only after that the judgment of God the great tribulation come to judge the earth.

The second reasons: "We find in the Scripture the church was not appointed to the wrath of God. "But let us who are of the day be sober; putting on the breastplate of faith and love, and as a helmet the hope of salvation. For God did not appoint us to wrath but to obtain salvation through our Lord Jesus Christ who died for us, that whether we wake or sleep we should live together with Him."

1 Th 5:8-10.

If the Rapture will be suddenly we must always live in holiness, that when He will come for us to be ready. Paul again says: "For the grace of God that brings salvation has appeared to all men, teaching us that, denying ungodliness and worldly lusts, we should live soberly, righteously and godly in the present age, looking for the blessed hope and glorious appearing of our great God and Savior Jesus Christ, and who gave Himself for us, that He might redeem us from every lawless deed and purify for Himself His own special people, zealous for good works. Speak these things, exhort, and rebuke with all authority. Let no one despise you."

Tit 2:11-15.

Jesus says: "But take heed to yourselves, lest your hearts be weighed down with carousing, drunkenness, and care of this life, and that Day come on you unexpectedly. For it will come as a snare on all those who dwell on the face of the whole earth. Watch therefore, and pray always that you may be counted worthy to escape all these things that will come to pass and to stand before the Son of Man."

Lk 21:34-36.

Are you ready?

Amen!

"I am the resurrection and the life. He who believes in Me, though he may die he shall live. And whoever lives and believes in Me shall never die. Do you believe this?"

John 11:25-26.

Chapter 15

A Word of Exhortation

> "Most assuredly, I say to you, He who hears My word and believes in Him who send Me has everlasting life, and shall not come into judgement, but has passed from death into life."
>
> John 5:24

Sure would be other things to write about, the great tribulation, the coming of the Lord on earth, the establishment of a thoU.S.nd years of peace on earth, about the second resurrection when all the people will go on trial, the new Jerusalem, but this may be in another time or in another book if is God will, now before closing I just want to give few words of exhortation to you my readers. My dear reader, after reading this book which is a part of my life experience lived by faith I take the courage directed by the Holy Spirit to ask you about yourself: Where are you coming from? Where are you now? Where are you going?

1. **For the One Who Don't Know God**

You have heared about God from your parents or friends but you don't pay to much attention to them, maybe because of what you learn in school about evolution or other science theory, or you hear that the Christians have a lots of restriction and you want to live your life how you please. But now you are at the point in life as I was when I told myself my life has no meaning, if so, I can tell you based on the word of God and my experience that is a sign that the life really begin for you now.

You did not come to this earth by chance, life is a gift from God, He is the Creator and if you are hire you are for a reason: If you are sick the Lord Jesus is your doctor, if you are poor the Lord Jesus is rich and He take care of you, if you are disappointed the Lord Jesus will give you peace and joy, if your friend or a wife or a husband or children's leaving you, the Lord is your true friend, if you are in jail maybe unfairly judge the Lord want to prepare you for the work you are called later, if you fall in temptation to sin and now you are addicted to drink, smoke, drug, immorality, pornography and any other thing, and you cannot leave them, God can deliver you. No matter in what situation you are my dear, I have a good news for you, God love you, and that what He tell us in the Bible:

"For God so loved the world that He gave His only begotten Son, that whoever believes in Him should not perish but have everlasting life."

John 3:16.

Now when you see that God loves you, that He gave His only Son to die for you to get forgiveness; what you need to do? If after this confession your heart was move by faith, the first thing you need to do is to repent, to admit that you are wrong to be sorry for what you did and ask God to forgive you, next you need to make covenant with God through the water baptism, and God will baptize you with the Holy Spirit which will help you to do the will of God in your life. Right now don't wait, seat down on your knees confess your sin before God and ask Him to forgive you, ask Him to help you there where you are, He is ready to forgive you to help you in any circumstance you are and give you salvation hire and in final eternal life. Find a good Evangelical Church and tell them that you want to make a covenant with God in the water baptism, and ask them if they have a Bible for you if not go and by one from Christian store, start to read the Bible every day and is better to start with the New Testament, ask Him to give guidance through the Holy Spirit.

2. For the One, Who Knows God, But Fall

If you believe in God and repented, even you are baptized but something happened in your life you was not strong enof and you fall into temptation of sin, and you are in the point of your life that you don't know if God can forgive you anymore and cannot rise up by yourself.

I want to tell you something no one is perfect righteous without sin only Jesus. We are all sinners, but we are sinners saved, if we make a mistake we come before God and ask Him to forgive us and don't sin no more. So what we need to do? That reading this book is not a random, God allowed to reach the book to be in your hand right now because He love you and give you a second chance.

You remember the story of Jonah from the Bible? He was a prophet of God and receive a revelation from God to go to Nineveh a big city in that time, and cry out against it because of their wickedness He supposed to go to Nineveh and tell them to repent if not God will destroy the city. But Jonah instead to go to Nineveh he chose to go to Tarshish and disobey the word of God for some reasons. God found Him and allow a great wind on the sea and the mariners was afraid, and cast the lots to find out the cause of this trouble, and the lots fell on Jonah. After he tell them what happened he said to them, throw me into the see and the see will became calm but God send a great fish to swallow him and stay there three days and three nights in the belly of the fish to repent and ask God for forgiveness and God save him and give him a second chance and the Lord spoke to the fish which vomited him out.

> "Now the word of the Lord come to Jonah the <u>second</u> time saying: Arise go to Nineveh that great city and preach to it the message I tell you. So Jonah arose and went to Nineveh, according to the word of the Lord. Now Nineveh was a exceedingly great city a three day journey in extent. And Jonah began to enter the city on the first day's walk. Then he cried out and said; "Yet forty days and Nineveh shall be overthrown" So the people of Nineveh believed God, proclaimed a fest and put on sackcloth from the greatest to the least of them."
>
> Jonah 3:1-5.

God teaches him a lessons to repent but in the same time give him a second chance to do the will of God, and after his preaching to Nineveh the people repent of their sin obey God which forgive them.

ExAmene your life and see where you sinned, confess your sin and left him, search the Scripture daily, speak with God in prayer, attend the church, unite with people of faith to grow spiritually and receive power. If you already receive peace and joy again you are on the right track, do not let the Lord, and He will not let you, the Bible says:

> "For He Himself has said, I will never leave you nor forsake you."
>
> Heb 13:5-b.

3. For the One Who is a Deceiver

You attend the church and made the baptism for other reasons, to marry a good girl or a good boy from the church, or urged by parents, or to win the Christian majority votes in political arena, whatever they may be, and you don't even give great importance to it in that time. You go to church but you are on the cross road and don't know what to do, you love your family and now fear God for what you did. Of course, all of these was wrong you can lie people but you cannot lie God, He know every things, He allow all of these to happen with a reason.

You hear the story of the Old Testament when Isaac had two twins boys the first he call him Esau and the second Jacob. After they grow up Esau become a skillful hunter and Jacob help his parents around the house. One time Esau come from the field and was very hungry and ask Jacob to give him some of his food. He take advantage of that and ask Esau to sell him his birthright, and because he was very hungry he sell it to Jacob. The second time when his father was old and cannot see he call his son Esau and ask him to go on field and hunt something for him and make him a good food and he will bless him before he die.

Rebeca his mother hear the conversation and because she like Jacob she teach him to bring her two of the baby goats to make a food that Isaac like. After that she dress him with Esau clothes and put the skin of the baby goats on his hands and send him to his father with the food. His father don't recognize him because he don't see, and his hands was like Esau hands and his clothes smelled like Esau clothes and he bless him. Not after long Esau come and prepare food like the father like and take it to his father. He find out that Jacob still his blessing:

> "But he said, your brother come with deceit and has taken away your blessing. And Esau said, is he not rightly named Jacob? For he has supplanted me these two times. He took away my birthright, and now look he has taken away my blessing!
>
> Gen 27:35-36.

Esau heart was full with hated because of that and he water for his father to die, and then he want to kill his Brother Jacob. Rebeca know what Esau have in plan and teach Jacob to flee to her Brother Laban in Haran. When he was on the way out from Beersheba one night he have a vision:

> "Then he dreamed and behold a ladder was set up on the earth and its top reached to heaven and there the angels of God were ascending and descending on it. And behold the Lord stood above it and said: I am the Lord God of Abraham your father and the God of Isaac,

the land on which you lie I will give to you and your descendants. Also your descendants shall be as the dust of the earth, you shall spread abroad to the west and the east to the north and the south, and in you and in your seed all the families of earth shall be blessed. Behold I am with you and will keep you wherever you go, and will bring you back to this land; for I will not leave you until I have done what I have spoken to you."

Gen 28:12-15.

Even that Jacob took the firstborn right and the blessing the wrong way but he obey his parents and he have fear of God for what he did, and God revealed to him all the blessing what he have in plan for him and for his seeds.

I just let you know you already made a covenant with God your creator He saw you and now He is waiting for you. Stop running you need one more thing to repent ask God for forgiveness and make peace with Him, today is your day to return to God. If you do this you will be bless you will fill release and you get direction like Jacob, and you will receive joy in your life hire on earth and in final eternal life.

4. For a Real Christian

You got faith and repentance and God has clothed with His power He gave you a gift, or more and now you enjoying His presence and working with joy in His church. Never forget my dear that you are here because of God and He give you the wisdom, He give you power, He give you the gift and He alone deserve the glory. It is sad but there are many who after years in the work of the Lord began to forget this, and tried to scalp

His credit and being tempted by the spirit of pride that led them to fall.

So whatever you are, you receive the anointing from the Holy Spirit, check the daily life, stay in fasting, fasting help you not to gorge and kip your body in its grip, stay in prayer, prayer help you to stay close to God and fill His presence, try to honor others ministers this will help them grow and help you to stay humble, study the word it help you grow spiritually and help you see how God see things, don't mess with the things of the world for many who have done this have receive a spirit of greed and have suffered the loss of faith, watching over your family which God give it to you, family is one God the most important things in the field of evangelism, which some in negligence have suffered the loss of it and they lost the ministry to.

In one word, you need to live a life of a balance, and do not give the devil any opportunity, you need to be a light in the darkness that God can use you for His work. I have a great joy for you and say God bless you and help you to the end. The word give you a beautiful promise:

> "Because you have kept My command to persevere .I also will keep you from the hour of trial which shall come upon the whole world to test those who dwell on earth. Behold I am coming quickly. Hold fast what you have, that no one may take your crown."
>
> Rev 3:10-11.

5. For a "Religious" Person

Now my thought is guided by the Holy Spirit to the one person which was born in one religion or he joined her later in life for various reasons, and now you are in on the point in life that you are not happy with it and you ask why is so many religions, and which one is the true religion. First of all to be clear from the start this is wrong. God did not make religions He give us one faith to serve Him, people made religions, they took one part of the Scripture upon which they based their doctrine of faith .

You can search about any religion and find out when was start and who was the founder of it. If you are born in one religion that is not mean it has to be good, your duty is to investigate to find the truth and not be lost. If you or your parents or even the country in which you were born was forced to accept a certain religion this should be a warning for you to investigate the truth. One thing that God does not do is to force anyone to serve Him.

He want you to serve Him by love. Due to ignorance or unbelief in God or lack of God word, or people was manipulate by their leaders and educated in this ideology or obliged and agreed to it like everyone else. Are even countries that where conquered in war and was forced to get the new religion if not they will be punish by death and overnight the country was changed. This is not the will of God that is the reason you have these questions in your heart.

Now if religions were made by people, we realize that the religion cannot be perfect, that is the reason these religions have turned their faith and the heart of the people to all kinds of gods which they don't have no power. Even if there are so many religions in the world and so many gods this make me believe that there is one a true religion and a true belief in God the Creator. It is sad that for many, the religion he was born with and the person who founded that religion is more important than God Himself and they don't listen to you or to investigate the true, either because of the laws that are very harsh in some country's with the death punishment, or because his religion tell him if he study other religion is a sin, or very simple that he receive and that he believe. Just the fact that you put these questions is a proof that God visit you and wants you to know the true faith and receive the true and to know Him and serve Him, and not only a religion.

To know the true first you need to get the Bible which is the word of God, and you need to start reading it because in it you will find the truth. Before God, is not wrong to investigate other religions and to test God and if you are sincere He will reviled to you so the Lord keep you, He enlighten you to give you wisdom to know and to understand the truth that made you free. If you find the true try to get connected with the people of faith to get close with God to know Him more and He will draw near to you and He will bless you in a way you cannot imagine and give you eternal life. Do not forget if you find the true faith and God was reviled to you, now you have a great debt to confess this to your family and your loved one, that they must find the true and God. I pray to the Lord to help you and bless you with everything you need to serve the true God.

6. For the People of God Israel

I can say that I have an esteem and respect in my heart for the people of God Israel that after them we receive the faith. If you are born Jew or adhered to this belief and now you see the state of Israel people, you see the hate of the neighbors grows increasingly more against the country and now you have so many questions that have no answer. If you are sincerely for God and want to find the answer I suggest you to read the New

Testament. Sure I could say many things about our Lord Jesus, about His birth, His life, His death and resurrection, and His disciples, but all of this you will find in the Holy Scripture. But I have a though that I want to share with you: Although at first the disciples where filled with fear, but after receiving the promised of the Holy Spirit now apostles received power and began to preach this Jesus whom they saw raised at the risk of their lives.

We find in Acts that God lids the word with signs and wonders:

> "And through the hands of the apostles many signs and wonders were done among the people. And they were all with one accord in Solomon's Porch. Yet none of the rest dared join them, but the people esteemed them highly. And believers were increasingly added to the Lord, multitudes of both man and women, so that they brought the sick out into the streets and laid them on the bedsand couches, that at least the shadow of Peter passing by might fall on some of them."
>
> Acts 5:12-16.

This aroused jealousy and the high priest and Sadducees game, laid hands on the apostles and put them in prison, but an angel of the Lord opened the prison doors and broth them out at night and they as their said to the angel, and went early in the morning in the temple and teaching the people. They were all amazed and did not know what to think but still the captain and officers of the temple and take a shower and brought before the council to judge, but some were determined to kill them. God did that in the midst was a Pharisee named Gamaliel, a teacher of the law.

"Then one in the council stood up a Pharisee named Gamaliel, a teacher of the law held in respect by all the people, and commanded them to put the apostles outside for a little while. And he said to them; Men of Israel, take heed to yourselves what you intend to do regarding these men. For some time ago Theudas rose up clamming to be somebody. A number of men, about four hundred, joined him. He was slain, and all who obeyed him were scattered and come to nothing. After this man, Judas of Galilee rose up in the days of the census, and drew away many people after him, He also perished, and all who obeyed him were dispersed. And now I say to you, keep away from these men and let them alone for it this plan or this work is of men it will come to nothing; but if it from God, you cannot overthrow it lest you even be found to fight against God. And they agreed with him, and when they called for the apostles and beaten them, they commanded that they should not speak in the name of Jesus, and let them go. So they departed from the presence of the council, rejoicing that they were counted worthy to suffer shame for His name. And daily in the temple and in every house, they did not cease teaching and preaching Jesus as the Christ."

Acts 5:34-42.

There is no greater miracle then that, after more than 2000 years, the faith of the apostles remained standing as proof that it is from God. Millions and millions of people have received faith in God and they receive the Lord Jesus as Savior of their life. Look around the faith in our Lord Jesus went in all countries, even in countries where faith is forbidden and is punished with death. In many stadiums are preaching, churches are not able to contain the crowd and tens of thousands worship God and worship His Name. Don't tell you something. The answer we have in the Bible. Once God has spoken through the prophet Ezekiel:

> "Say to them, As I live, says the Lord God, I have no pleasure in the death of the wicked, but that the wicked turn from his way and live, Turn, turn from your evil ways! For why should you die, O house of Israel?"
>
> Ezek 33:11.

One thing you lack of both for yourself as well as the entire people of Israel; to return to God and repent and to receive the Lord Jesus Christ as Messiah, for only Him can give you peace. God is ready to forgive you to accept you are you ready? And the grace of our Lord Jesus Christ and the love of God and the fellowship of the Holy Spirit be with you all.

Amen!

> "And the Spirit and the bride say, Come! And let him who hear say, Come! And let him who thirsts come. Whoever desires, let him take the water of life freely."
>
> Rev 22:17.

My mother

After prayer meeting in Latina Italy

Worship with my brothers in Phoenix Arizona 1983

First prayer meeting at CFTNI campus in the summer of 1984

Dallas Romanian Penticostal Church meeting

With my wife at my graduation from CFNI in 1986

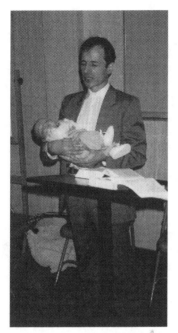

First dedication in Romanian Penticostal Church

Brothers meeting at Dallas Penticostal Church

In parking lot after church service

First water baptism in Dallas Romanian Penticostal Church

One of the first missions to Weco Texas

Water baptism in Weco Texas

First mission to Hateg Romania in 1992

First mission to Dunareni Romania in 1994

World Evangelism Ministry
Contact Information

U.S.A

P. O. Box 381503
Duncanville, TX 75138

Romania

Str- Horea, Nr- 27, Loc- Hateg,
Jud- Hunedoara, Romania, Europe

Or visit us on the web at:
World-Evangelism-Ministry.org
info@world-evangelism-ministry.org

Please, support our Ministry by ordering books and making donations that will go 100% to the ministry.

Thank you, and God bless you.

Printed in the United States
By Bookmasters